Apress Pocket Guides

Apress Pocket Guides present concise summaries of cutting-edge developments and working practices throughout the tech industry. Shorter in length, books in this series aims to deliver quick-to-read guides that are easy to absorb, perfect for the time-poor professional.

This series covers the full spectrum of topics relevant to the modern industry, from security, AI, machine learning, cloud computing, web development, product design, to programming techniques and business topics too.

Typical topics might include:

- A concise guide to a particular topic, method, function or framework
- Professional best practices and industry trends
- A snapshot of a hot or emerging topic
- Industry case studies
- Concise presentations of core concepts suited for students and those interested in entering the tech industry
- Short reference guides outlining 'need-to-know' concepts and practices.

More information about this series at `https://link.springer.com/bookseries/17385`.

From Source to Shelf

Orchestrating a Supply Chain Symphony

Viraj Lele
Yash Ajmeri

Apress®

From Source to Shelf: Orchestrating a Supply Chain Symphony

Viraj Lele
Philadelphia, PA, USA

Yash Ajmeri
Philadelphia, PA, USA

ISBN-13 (pbk): 979-8-8688-0985-9
https://doi.org/10.1007/979-8-8688-0986-6

ISBN-13 (electronic): 979-8-8688-0986-6

Copyright © 2024 by Viraj Lele, Yash Ajmeri

This work is subject to copyright. All rights are reserved by the Publisher, whether the whole or part of the material is concerned, specifically the rights of translation, reprinting, reuse of illustrations, recitation, broadcasting, reproduction on microfilms or in any other physical way, and transmission or information storage and retrieval, electronic adaptation, computer software, or by similar or dissimilar methodology now known or hereafter developed.

Trademarked names, logos, and images may appear in this book. Rather than use a trademark symbol with every occurrence of a trademarked name, logo, or image we use the names, logos, and images only in an editorial fashion and to the benefit of the trademark owner, with no intention of infringement of the trademark.

The use in this publication of trade names, trademarks, service marks, and similar terms, even if they are not identified as such, is not to be taken as an expression of opinion as to whether or not they are subject to proprietary rights.

While the advice and information in this book are believed to be true and accurate at the date of publication, neither the authors nor the editors nor the publisher can accept any legal responsibility for any errors or omissions that may be made. The publisher makes no warranty, express or implied, with respect to the material contained herein.

> Managing Director, Apress Media LLC: Welmoed Spahr
> Acquisitions Editor: Shivangi Ramachandran
> Development Editor: James Markham
> Project Manager: Jessica Vakili

Distributed to the book trade worldwide by Springer Science+Business Media New York, 1 New York Plaza, New York, NY 10004. Phone 1-800-SPRINGER, fax (201) 348-4505, e-mail orders-ny@springer-sbm.com, or visit www.springeronline.com. Apress Media, LLC is a California LLC and the sole member (owner) is Springer Science + Business Media Finance Inc (SSBM Finance Inc). SSBM Finance Inc is a **Delaware** corporation.

For information on translations, please e-mail booktranslations@springernature.com; for reprint, paperback, or audio rights, please e-mail bookpermissions@springernature.com.

Apress titles may be purchased in bulk for academic, corporate, or promotional use. eBook versions and licenses are also available for most titles. For more information, reference our Print and eBook Bulk Sales web page at http://www.apress.com/bulk-sales.

If disposing of this product, please recycle the paper

To the almighty, my parents, and my spiritual master, whose unwavering love and support have been the foundation of all my endeavors. Your belief in me has given me the strength and courage to pursue my passions.

To my colleagues, whose collaboration and encouragement have shaped my journey. Your insights and shared experiences have been invaluable in my growth.

Acknowledging Gary Roberts—thank you for your mentorship and the incredible opportunities you've provided. Your guidance has been instrumental in my development within the field of supply chain, and I am forever grateful for the trust you've placed in me.

This book is for all of you.

— Viraj Lele

— Yash Ajmeri

Table of Contents

About the Authors .... **xv**

Acknowledgments .... **xvii**

Chapter 1: Introduction to Supply Chain Management **1**

   1.1 Understanding the Supply Chain 4

   1.2 Key Concepts and Definitions 5

   1.3 Evolution of Supply Chain Management 7

   1.4 The Role of Technology in Supply Chain Management 10

   1.5 Case Studies: Successful Supply Chain Implementations 12

      The Challenge 14

      The Strategy 15

      The Results 17

      Conclusion 17

      The Challenge 18

      The Strategy 18

      The Results 20

Chapter 2: Production Planning and Control **23**

   2.1 Fundamentals of Production Planning 25

      Efficient Resource Allocation 26

      Dynamic Production Scheduling 26

   2.2 Demand Forecasting Techniques 26

      Leveraging Machine Learning for Demand Forecasting 27

      Harnessing Big Data for Real-Time Insights 27

TABLE OF CONTENTS

Predictive Analytics for Strategic Decision-Making 28
The Role of Collaborative Forecasting 28
Scenario Planning for Demand Uncertainty 29
2.3 Inventory Management 29
The Essence of Inventory Management 30
Just-in-Time (JIT) Inventory Management 30
Integrating Technology for Real-Time Inventory Tracking 31
Demand-Driven Inventory Optimization 31
Sustainable Inventory Management Practices 32
The Role of Automation in Inventory Management 32
2.4 Capacity Planning 33
Understanding Capacity Planning 33
Techniques for Effective Capacity Planning 34
Strategic Investment in Capacity Expansion 35
Balancing Flexibility and Efficiency 35
Continuous Improvement Through Data-Driven Insights 36
2.5 Production Scheduling and Control 36
The Essence of Production Scheduling 36
Strategies for Effective Production Scheduling 37
Real-Time Monitoring and Control 38
Lean Manufacturing Principles in Production Scheduling 38
Integration of Advanced Technologies 39
Continuous Improvement and Adaptability 39
2.6 Lean Manufacturing Principles 40
Elimination of Waste: The Foundation of Lean 40
Continuous Improvement (Kaizen) 41

Respect for People 42
Pull Production Systems.. 42
Value Stream Mapping 42

Chapter 3: Logistics and Distribution Management 45

3.1 Overview of Logistics Management... 48
    The Role and Importance of Logistics Management 48
    Key Components of Logistics Management 49
    The Impact of Technology on Logistics Management.................... 52

3.2 Transportation Management 53
    The Strategic Importance of Transportation Management 53
    Key Components of Transportation Management......................... 54
    The Role of Technology in Transportation Management............... 58

3.3 Warehousing and Storage Solutions 60
    The Role of Warehousing in the Supply Chain 61
    Types of Warehousing Solutions.. 61
    Innovations in Warehousing: The Future of Storage Solutions 63
    Real-World Applications: Success Stories in Warehousing 65

3.4 Distribution Network Design 66
    The Strategic Importance of Distribution Network Design 67
    Key Factors Influencing Distribution Network Design 68
    Methodologies for Designing Distribution Networks 69
    Real-World Examples of Successful Distribution Network Design 71
    The Impact of Emerging Technologies on Distribution Network Design......... 72

3.5 Third-Party Logistics (3PL) and Fourth-Party Logistics (4PL)....... 73
    Understanding Third-Party Logistics (3PL) 73
    The Evolution of Fourth-Party Logistics (4PL) 74
    Examples of 3PL and 4PL Success.. 76
    The Future of 3PL and 4PL 76

TABLE OF CONTENTS

3.6 Reverse Logistics 77
    The Growing Importance of Reverse Logistics 78
    Key Components of Reverse Logistics 78
    Challenges in Reverse Logistics 81
    Innovative Strategies in Reverse Logistics 81
    The Future of Reverse Logistics 82

Chapter 4: Supply Chain Integration and Collaboration 83

4.1 The Importance of Supply Chain Integration 84
4.2 Strategies for Achieving Supply Chain Integration 85
4.3 The Role of Collaboration in Supply Chain Integration 87
4.4 Benefits of Supply Chain Integration and Collaboration 87
4.5 The Importance of Integration in Supply Chains 89
    Driving Efficiency Through Integration 90
    Reducing Costs and Enhancing Profitability 90
    Enhancing Agility and Responsiveness 91
    Fostering Innovation and Competitive Advantage 92
    The Future of Supply Chain Integration 92
4.6 Collaborative Planning, Forecasting, and Replenishment (CPFR) 93
    The Essence of CPFR 94
    Improving Demand Forecasting Accuracy 94
    Enhancing Supply Chain Agility 95
    Optimizing Inventory Management 96
    Strengthening Relationships and Trust 96
    The Future of CPFR 97
4.7 Supplier Relationship Management (SRM) 98
    The Strategic Importance of SRM 98
    Building Strong Supplier Relationships 99
    Driving Innovation through SRM 99

TABLE OF CONTENTS

    Enhancing Supplier Performance and Accountability.................100

    The Future of SRM: Digital Transformation..................................101

4.8 Information Sharing and Coordination 102

    The Strategic Importance of Information Sharing 103

    Overcoming Barriers to Information Sharing...............................104

    The Role of Technology in Enhancing Information Sharing 105

    The Impact of Information Sharing on Supply Chain Performance 106

    The Future of Information Sharing and Coordination 107

4.9 Risk Management in Supply Chains 107

    Understanding Supply Chain Risks...108

    Risk Identification and Assessment..108

    Risk Mitigation Strategies 109

    The Role of Technology in Supply Chain Risk Management.......110

    Building a Resilient Supply Chain...110

    The Future of Supply Chain Risk Management 111

4.10 Case Studies: Collaborative Supply Chain Success Stories 112

    Case Study 1: Unilever and Its Sustainable Agriculture Initiative 112

    Case Study 2: Walmart and P&G's Collaborative Planning, Forecasting, and Replenishment (CPFR) Initiative 113

    Case Study 3: Toyota and Its Just-in-Time (JIT) System with Suppliers......114

    Case Study 4: The Coca-Cola Company and Collaborative Logistics with Suppliers 115

    Case Study 5: IBM and Collaborative Innovation in Supply Chain Management..116

4.11 The Power of Collaboration in Supply Chain Success................117

Chapter 5: Future Trends and Innovations in Supply Chain Management..119

  5.1 Digital Supply Chains and the Role of Artificial Intelligence 120

  5.2 Blockchain Technology for Enhanced Transparency and Security.............121

TABLE OF CONTENTS

5.3 Sustainable Supply Chain Practices 121
5.4 The Rise of E-commerce and Omnichannel Supply Chains 122
5.5 Resilient and Agile Supply Chains 123
5.6 Embracing the Future of Supply Chain Management 124
5.7 The Impact of Artificial Intelligence and Machine Learning 124
    Enhanced Demand Forecasting and Inventory Management 125
    Optimized Logistics and Transportation 125
    Automated Quality Control and Defect Detection 126
    Supply Chain Risk Management and Resilience Building 127
    Enhanced Supplier Relationship Management 127
    Personalized Customer Experiences and Demand Shaping 128
    Ethical AI and Sustainable Supply Chain Practices 129
    The Future of AI and ML in Supply Chain Management 129
5.8 Blockchain Technology in Supply Chains 130
    Understanding Blockchain Technology in Supply Chains 130
    Enhancing Traceability and Transparency 131
    Improving Supply Chain Efficiency and Reducing Costs 131
    Combating Counterfeiting and Ensuring Product Authenticity 132
    Facilitating Smart Contracts and Automating Transactions 133
    Enhancing Supplier Relationship Management and Collaboration 134
    Addressing Regulatory Compliance and Sustainability Goals 134
    The Future of Blockchain in Supply Chain Management 135
5.9 The Role of Big Data and Analytics 135
    Understanding Big Data in Supply Chains 136
    Enhancing Demand Forecasting and Inventory Optimization 136
    Improving Supplier Relationship Management and Procurement 137
    Enhancing Transportation and Logistics Optimization 138
    Enhancing Risk Management and Resilience 139

Driving Customer-Centric Supply Chains 140

Leveraging Predictive and Prescriptive Analytics for Strategic
Decision-Making 141

The Future of Big Data and Analytics in Supply Chain Management 141

5.10 Sustainable Supply Chain Practices 142

The Importance of Sustainability in Supply Chains 142

Key Components of Sustainable Supply Chain Practices 143

Examples of Sustainable Supply Chain Practices 144

The Challenges of Implementing Sustainable Supply Chain Practices 146

The Future of Sustainable Supply Chains 147

5.11 The Future of E-commerce and Omnichannel Logistics 148

The Evolution of E-commerce and Consumer Expectations 148

Key Drivers of Omnichannel Logistics 149

The Role of Technology in Shaping the Future of
Omnichannel Logistics 150

Emerging Trends in E-commerce and Omnichannel Logistics 151

Examples of Companies Leading the Way in Omnichannel Logistics 152

Challenges and Opportunities in the Future of Omnichannel Logistics 153

5.12 Preparing for Future Disruptions in Supply Chains 154

Understanding the Landscape of Supply Chain Disruptions 155

Building a Resilient Supply Chain 156

Enhancing Flexibility in Supply Chain Operations 157

Leveraging Technology for Disruption Preparedness 158

Developing Robust Contingency Plans 159

The Role of Collaboration and Partnership in Mitigating Disruptions 160

Index 163

About the Authors

Viraj Lele is an esteemed Industrial Engineer and Business Unit Advisor, whose profound expertise and innovative approach have made him a leading figure in the realm of Supply Chain and Production Technologies. With a distinguished career marked by a deep understanding of supply chain dynamics and a strategic mindset, Viraj is at the forefront of optimizing and transforming logistics operations.

Yash A.: His journey in the financial services industry is a testament to dedication, growth, and a passion for helping individuals achieve their goals. Since starting his career over the years he has quickly developed a deep understanding of the fundamentals of market and service factors. His keen attention to detail led to his rapid advancements in his career in meeting the financial needs of businesses. Today, as a prominent figure in the finance and service sector, he leverages his extensive experience across various facets to offer comprehensive planning and management services.

Acknowledgments

We are deeply grateful to all the companies featured in this book. Their unwavering commitment to a growth mindset and action-driven approach have been truly inspiring. Their dedication to continuous improvement and innovation in the field of supply chain management has not only driven success but also serves as a valuable learning resource for aspiring professionals.

Their experiences, challenges, and strategies have provided invaluable insights that will undoubtedly benefit readers who seek to enhance their knowledge and skills in this dynamic field. Such contributions enrich books and will help foster the development of a new generation of supply chain leaders.

With deepest gratitude.

Disclaimer

The images used in the book are AI-generated cover versions. The publication and authors do not claim ownership or rights about the featured images. Insights from different companies mentioned in the book and all rights and information remain with the respective companies. The information is not intended to infringe on the rights and information of the companies.

The information presented in this book is for informational purposes only. While we have made every effort to ensure the accuracy and reliability of the information provided, we make no representations or warranties of any kind, express or implied, about the completeness, accuracy, reliability, suitability, or availability with respect to the book or the information contained within.

ACKNOWLEDGMENTS

All rights to the information shared about companies mentioned in this book belong solely to those respective companies. The authors or the publication claim no ownership of the information shared. All rights remain with the original companies, and the information is presented purely to demonstrate their lessons. It is not intended to infringe on the rights of the companies.

As authors and publishers, we accept no responsibility for any direct, indirect, implied, special, incidental, or consequential damages arising from any actions taken as a result of using the information provided in this book. Readers are advised to use their discretion and consult with their respective professionals before making any decisions or taking any actions based on the information in this book.

We cannot be held liable for any errors, omissions, or inaccuracies in the information provided. The views and opinions expressed in this book are those of the authors and do not necessarily reflect the official policy or position of any other individual, organization, or company.

Any reliance you place on the information in this book is strictly at your own risk. We do not guarantee the accuracy, reliability, or completeness of the information and disclaim any liability for any loss or damage incurred in connection with the use of this book.

Please consult with your respective professionals or experts for specific advice tailored to your individual needs and circumstances.

CHAPTER 1

Introduction to Supply Chain Management

Supply chain management (SCM) is the intricate process of overseeing the flow of goods, information, and finances as a product moves from the supplier to the manufacturer to the wholesaler to the retailer and finally to the consumer. SCM encompasses every aspect of production and logistics, making it a critical element for businesses striving to meet consumer demands efficiently and effectively. This chapter delves into the essential concepts of SCM, exploring its key elements, historical evolution, technological impacts, and real-world applications through detailed examples and case studies.

The supply chain is not just about moving products from point A to point B. It involves a complex web of interconnected activities, including procurement, production, transportation, warehousing, and distribution. Effective SCM can significantly reduce operational costs, improve customer satisfaction, and provide a competitive advantage in the market. For instance, companies like Amazon have built their business models around highly efficient and responsive supply chains, allowing them to offer rapid delivery services that have redefined consumer expectations.

CHAPTER 1   INTRODUCTION TO SUPPLY CHAIN MANAGEMENT

To fully appreciate the intricacies of SCM, it's crucial to understand the key concepts and terminologies that define the field. Terms such as lead time, just-in-time (JIT) inventory, and the bullwhip effect are foundational to SCM. These concepts help businesses optimize their supply chains by minimizing delays, reducing inventory costs, and preventing demand fluctuations from disrupting production schedules.

The evolution of SCM reflects the broader changes in global business practices and technological advancements. From the early days of localized supply chains to the current era of globalized networks, SCM has continually adapted to meet the changing needs of businesses and consumers. Innovations like Henry Ford's assembly line revolutionized manufacturing by significantly reducing production time and costs. Today, companies leverage advanced technologies such as artificial intelligence (AI), the Internet of Things (IoT), and blockchain to enhance supply chain efficiency, visibility, and security.

Technology plays a pivotal role in modern SCM, enabling companies to automate processes, improve accuracy, and respond quickly to market changes. AI-powered predictive analytics can forecast demand with high precision, allowing businesses to optimize inventory levels and reduce waste. IoT devices provide real-time tracking and monitoring of goods, ensuring they remain in optimal condition during transit. Blockchain technology offers a transparent and secure method for recording transactions, enhancing trust and collaboration among supply chain partners.

Let us consider some real-world scenarios. Real-world case studies provide valuable insights into how businesses successfully implement SCM strategies. For example, Zara, a global fashion retailer, has mastered the art of agile supply chain management. By maintaining tight control over its supply chain and closely monitoring fashion trends, Zara can design, produce, and deliver new styles to stores within weeks. This rapid response capability allows Zara to meet consumer demand swiftly and minimize excess inventory, giving it a significant competitive edge over traditional retailers.

CHAPTER 1   INTRODUCTION TO SUPPLY CHAIN MANAGEMENT

SCM is a multifaceted discipline that requires a deep understanding of various interconnected elements. This chapter provides a comprehensive overview of SCM, highlighting its importance in today's global economy. By examining key concepts, historical evolution, technological impacts, and successful case studies, readers will gain a solid foundation in SCM, preparing them for further exploration of this critical business function.

Figure 1-1. Overview of How Supply Chain Operations Work

3

CHAPTER 1   INTRODUCTION TO SUPPLY CHAIN MANAGEMENT

1.1 Understanding the Supply Chain

The supply chain is a network of entities, activities, and resources involved in producing and delivering a product from the supplier to the consumer. It includes raw material procurement, manufacturing, transportation, warehousing, and distribution. A well-coordinated supply chain ensures that products reach consumers in a timely and cost-effective manner, enhancing overall efficiency and customer satisfaction.

Consider the supply chain of a popular electronic device, such as a smartphone. The journey begins with sourcing raw materials like rare earth metals from mining companies. These materials are transported to component manufacturers, who produce various parts like processors, screens, and batteries. The components are then shipped to assembly plants, where the smartphone is assembled. Once assembled, the smartphones are distributed to warehouses, retail stores, and finally to consumers. Each step in this process requires meticulous planning and coordination to ensure timely delivery and quality maintenance.

Supply chains can vary significantly in complexity depending on the product and the number of stakeholders involved. A simple supply chain might involve just a few steps, such as a local bakery sourcing ingredients, baking goods, and selling them directly to customers. In contrast, a global supply chain, like that of an automobile manufacturer, involves numerous suppliers, manufacturers, and distributors across multiple countries, each contributing to the production and delivery of the final product.

Understanding the supply chain is crucial for identifying potential bottlenecks and inefficiencies. By mapping out the entire process, businesses can pinpoint areas where delays or cost overruns occur and implement strategies to address these issues. For instance, a company might find that transportation costs are significantly higher than expected due to inefficient routing. By optimizing its logistics network, it can reduce costs and improve delivery times.

Moreover, understanding the supply chain helps businesses manage risks more effectively. Supply chains are vulnerable to various disruptions, such as natural disasters, political instability, and supplier bankruptcies. By identifying potential risks and developing contingency plans, companies can mitigate the impact of these disruptions and ensure continuity of supply.

The supply chain is the backbone of modern businesses, connecting suppliers, manufacturers, distributors, and consumers. A deep understanding of the supply chain allows businesses to optimize their operations, reduce costs, improve customer satisfaction, and manage risks effectively. By focusing on each link in the chain, companies can create a seamless and efficient process that delivers value to both the business and its customers.

1.2 Key Concepts and Definitions

To navigate the complexities of supply chain management, it is essential to understand the key concepts and definitions that underpin the field. These concepts provide the framework for optimizing supply chain operations and achieving business objectives.

One of the fundamental concepts in SCM is **supply chain visibility**. This refers to the ability to track and monitor products in real time as they move through the supply chain. For example, a fashion retailer can use RFID tags to monitor inventory levels and product locations from suppliers to retail stores. This visibility allows the retailer to quickly respond to changes in demand, reduce stockouts, and enhance customer satisfaction.

Another critical concept is **lead time**, which is the total time it takes for a product to move from the initial order to the final delivery. Reducing lead time is essential for improving supply chain efficiency and responsiveness. For instance, a manufacturer that can reduce its lead time from six weeks to four weeks can respond more quickly to market changes and reduce inventory holding costs.

CHAPTER 1   INTRODUCTION TO SUPPLY CHAIN MANAGEMENT

Just-in-time (JIT) inventory is a strategy that aims to minimize inventory levels by aligning production and delivery schedules with the actual demand. By producing goods only when they are needed, businesses can reduce storage costs and minimize the risk of overproduction. For example, a car manufacturer using JIT inventory will produce specific car models only when there are confirmed orders, rather than maintaining a large inventory of unsold vehicles.

The **bullwhip effect** describes the phenomenon where small fluctuations in consumer demand lead to larger variations in orders placed along the supply chain. This can result in excess inventory, stockouts, and increased costs. For example, a slight increase in demand for a product can cause retailers to order more from wholesalers, who in turn order even larger quantities from manufacturers. To mitigate the bullwhip effect, businesses can improve communication and collaboration with supply chain partners, use better forecasting techniques, and implement demand-driven supply chain strategies.

Inventory management is another vital concept, involving the optimization of inventory levels to meet customer demand while minimizing costs. Effective inventory management ensures that the right products are available at the right time and place. For instance, an e-commerce company can use advanced inventory management software to track stock levels, predict demand, and automate reordering processes.

Understanding key SCM concepts and definitions is crucial for optimizing supply chain operations. By leveraging supply chain visibility, reducing lead time, implementing JIT inventory, mitigating the bullwhip effect, and optimizing inventory management, businesses can enhance efficiency, reduce costs, and improve customer satisfaction.

1.3 Evolution of Supply Chain Management

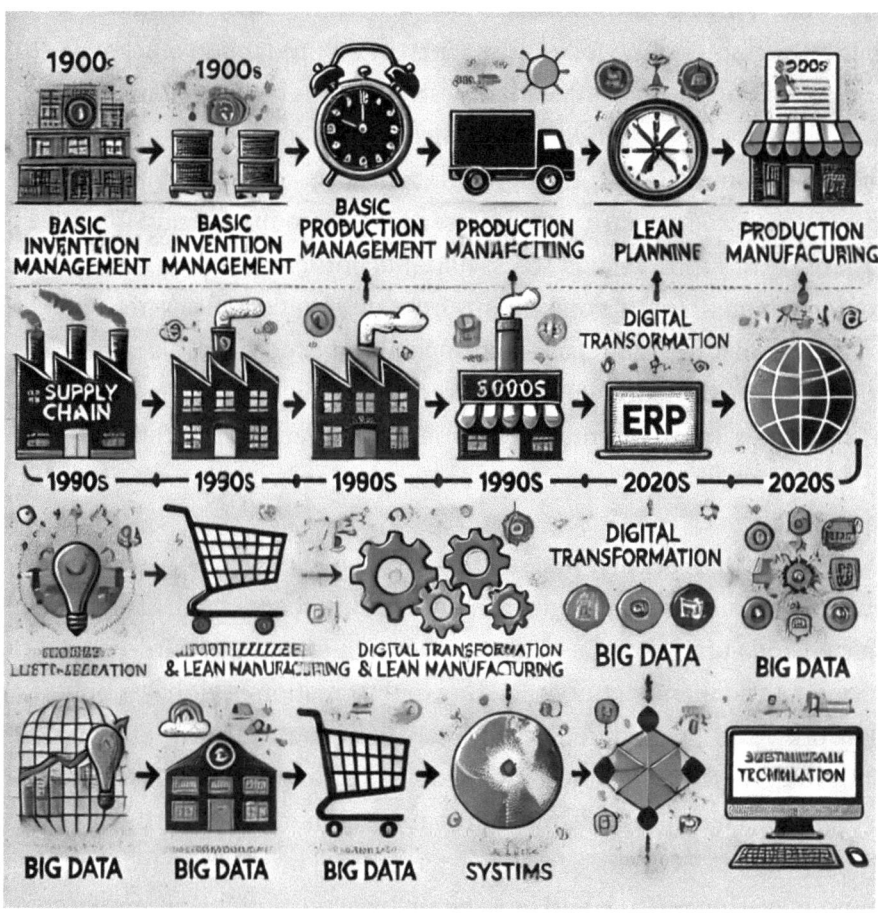

Figure 1-2. *Evolution of Supply Chain Management*

The evolution of supply chain management reflects the broader changes in global business practices and technological advancements. From the early days of localized supply chains to the current era of globalized networks, SCM has continually adapted to meet the changing needs of businesses and consumers.

CHAPTER 1   INTRODUCTION TO SUPPLY CHAIN MANAGEMENT

In the early 20th century, supply chains were relatively simple and localized. Companies typically sourced raw materials from nearby suppliers, manufactured products in-house, and sold them directly to local customers. The focus was primarily on production efficiency and cost reduction. A significant milestone in this era was Henry Ford's introduction of the assembly line, which revolutionized manufacturing by significantly reducing production time and costs.

The mid-20th century saw the rise of mass production and the expansion of supply chains across national borders. Companies began sourcing materials and components from different countries to take advantage of lower labor costs and specialized expertise. This period also witnessed the development of new transportation and communication technologies, such as container shipping and telecommunication networks, which facilitated the movement of goods and information across long distances.

The late 20th century marked the advent of globalization, with supply chains becoming increasingly complex and interconnected. Companies started outsourcing various aspects of their operations to third-party suppliers and manufacturers, leading to the creation of global supply networks. The focus shifted from merely reducing costs to optimizing the entire supply chain for efficiency, flexibility, and responsiveness.

In the 21st century, technological advancements have further transformed SCM. Innovations such as artificial intelligence (AI), the Internet of Things (IoT), and blockchain have revolutionized supply chain operations. AI-powered predictive analytics can forecast demand with high accuracy, allowing businesses to optimize inventory levels and reduce waste. IoT devices provide real-time tracking and monitoring of goods, ensuring they remain in optimal condition during transit. Blockchain technology offers a transparent and secure method for recording transactions, enhancing trust and collaboration among supply chain partners.

CHAPTER 1   INTRODUCTION TO SUPPLY CHAIN MANAGEMENT

A notable example of modern SCM is Amazon's logistics network. By leveraging advanced technologies and innovative strategies, Amazon has built one of the most efficient and responsive supply chains in the world. The company's use of robotics in warehouses, predictive analytics for demand forecasting, and sophisticated routing algorithms for delivery optimization have enabled it to offer services like same-day delivery, setting new standards in the industry.

The evolution of SCM has also been driven by changing consumer expectations. Today's consumers demand greater product variety, higher quality, and faster delivery times. To meet these expectations, companies must continuously innovate and adapt their supply chain strategies. This involves not only leveraging new technologies but also adopting practices such as sustainable sourcing, ethical manufacturing, and circular supply chains to address environmental and social concerns.

The evolution of supply chain management reflects the dynamic nature of global business and technological progress. From the early days of localized supply chains to the current era of globalized networks and advanced technologies, SCM has continually evolved to meet the changing needs of businesses and consumers. Understanding this evolution provides valuable insights into the challenges and opportunities of modern supply chain management.

CHAPTER 1   INTRODUCTION TO SUPPLY CHAIN MANAGEMENT

1.4 The Role of Technology in Supply Chain Management

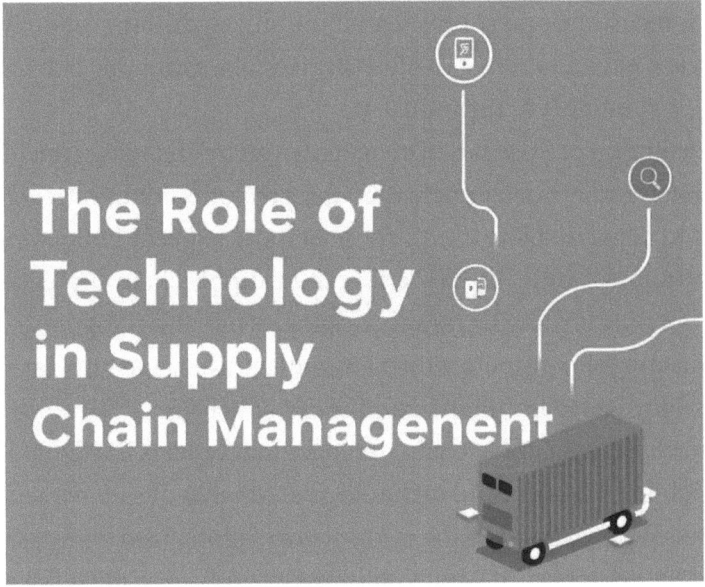

Figure 1-3. The Role of Technology in Supply Chain Management

Technology has become a cornerstone of modern supply chain management, enabling companies to enhance efficiency, accuracy, and responsiveness. Innovations such as artificial intelligence (AI), the Internet of Things (IoT), and blockchain are transforming supply chains by automating processes, improving visibility, and securing transactions.

Artificial intelligence (AI) is revolutionizing supply chain management by providing powerful tools for demand forecasting, inventory optimization, and decision-making. AI-powered predictive analytics can analyze vast amounts of data from various sources, such as sales records, market trends, and social media, to predict future demands with high

CHAPTER 1   INTRODUCTION TO SUPPLY CHAIN MANAGEMENT

accuracy. For example, a grocery retailer can use AI to forecast demand for perishable goods, ensuring that it stocks the right quantities and minimize waste.

The Internet of Things (IoT) is another game-changer in SCM. IoT devices, such as smart sensors and RFID tags, can track and monitor products in real time as they move through the supply chain. This real-time visibility allows businesses to monitor the condition of goods during transit, detect potential issues early, and take corrective actions promptly. For instance, a pharmaceutical company can use IoT sensors to monitor the temperature and humidity of vaccines during transportation, ensuring they remain within safe limits and maintain their efficacy.

Blockchain technology is enhancing supply chain security and transparency. Blockchain provides a decentralized and immutable ledger for recording transactions, making it nearly impossible to alter or tamper with data. This transparency and security are particularly valuable in industries where trust and authenticity are critical, such as the food and pharmaceutical sectors. For example, a food manufacturer can use blockchain to trace the origin and journey of its products from farm to table, ensuring that consumers receive safe and authentic goods.

Robotics and automation are also playing a significant role in modern supply chains. Automated systems can handle repetitive tasks with high precision and speed, reducing labor costs and minimizing human errors. In warehouses, robots can pick, pack, and sort products efficiently, while autonomous vehicles can transport goods between facilities. For example, Amazon uses a fleet of robots in its fulfillment centers to streamline order processing and improve operational efficiency.

Advanced analytics and big data are providing deeper insights into supply chain performance. By analyzing data from various sources, businesses can identify patterns, trends, and anomalies that might otherwise go unnoticed. This information can inform strategic decisions, such as optimizing inventory levels, improving supplier performance, and enhancing customer service. For instance, a retail chain can use big data analytics to analyze customer purchase behavior and optimize product assortments in different stores.

In summary, technology is transforming supply chain management by automating processes, improving visibility, and enhancing security. AI, IoT, blockchain, robotics, and advanced analytics are enabling businesses to optimize their supply chains, reduce costs, and meet consumer demands more effectively. By leveraging these technologies, companies can create more agile, responsive, and resilient supply chains that provide a competitive edge in today's dynamic market.

1.5 Case Studies: Successful Supply Chain Implementations

Real-world case studies provide valuable insights into how companies have successfully implemented supply chain management strategies to achieve their business goals. These examples illustrate the practical applications of SCM concepts and highlight the benefits of effective supply chain management.

One of the most notable examples of successful SCM implementation is Zara. Zara's business model is built on the ability to quickly respond to changing fashion trends and deliver new styles to stores within weeks. This rapid response capability is achieved through a combination of tight supply chain control, efficient production processes, and strategic logistics.

Zara maintains close relationships with its suppliers and manufacturers, allowing it to coordinate production and delivery schedules tightly. The company uses a mix of in-house manufacturing and outsourcing to balance cost and flexibility. By keeping production in close proximity to its headquarters in Spain, Zara can quickly adjust its production plans based on real-time sales data and market trends.

CHAPTER 1   INTRODUCTION TO SUPPLY CHAIN MANAGEMENT

Another key element of Zara's supply chain strategy is its focus on small batch production. Instead of producing large quantities of each style, Zara manufactures smaller batches, which reduces the risk of excess inventory and allows the company to introduce new designs more frequently. This approach also creates a sense of urgency among customers, encouraging them to make purchases quickly before items run out of stock.

Zara's distribution network is designed for speed and efficiency. The company uses a centralized distribution center in Spain to process and ship products to its stores worldwide. Advanced logistics systems and automated sorting technologies enable Zara to rapidly dispatch orders, ensuring that stores receive new merchandise twice a week. This frequent replenishment keeps Zara's inventory fresh and aligns with the fast-paced nature of the fashion industry.

Another compelling case study is Amazon, a global leader in e-commerce and logistics. Amazon's supply chain strategy is built on the principles of speed, efficiency, and customer-centricity. The company's extensive network of fulfillment centers, sophisticated inventory management systems, and advanced logistics capabilities enable it to offer services like same-day and next-day delivery.

Amazon's fulfillment centers are equipped with state-of-the-art robotics and automation technologies, which streamline order processing and improve operational efficiency. Robots handle tasks such as picking, packing, and sorting, while automated guided vehicles transport goods within the warehouse. These technologies not only reduce labor costs but also minimize errors and accelerate order fulfillment.

Amazon's use of predictive analytics and machine learning further enhances its supply chain efficiency. By analyzing vast amounts of data, Amazon can forecast demand accurately, optimize inventory levels, and anticipate potential disruptions. For example, during peak shopping periods like Black Friday and Cyber Monday, Amazon uses predictive analytics to ensure it has sufficient stock of popular items and allocate resources effectively.

CHAPTER 1   INTRODUCTION TO SUPPLY CHAIN MANAGEMENT

A third example is Toyota, renowned for its implementation of the just-in-time (JIT) manufacturing system. Toyota's JIT approach focuses on producing only what is needed, when it is needed, and in the quantities needed. This strategy minimizes inventory levels, reduces waste, and enhances production efficiency.

Toyota's JIT system relies on close collaboration with suppliers and a well-coordinated production schedule. Suppliers deliver components just in time for assembly, reducing the need for large inventories and storage space. This approach requires precise planning and robust communication to ensure that components arrive on time and meet quality standards.

One more example is of a mid-sized electronics manufacturer headquartered in Asia that faced significant challenges in its supply chain that were threatening its market position. Rising costs, inefficient logistics, and poor supplier relationships were leading to missed delivery deadlines and declining customer satisfaction. This case study explores how the Corporation overhauled its supply chain to not only solve these problems but also to turn them into a competitive advantage, positioning the company as a leader in its industry.

The Challenge

The Corporation was experiencing rapid growth, expanding its product lines and entering new markets. However, its supply chain needed to be keeping pace with this expansion. The company relied heavily on multiple suppliers from different regions, leading to inconsistent quality and frequent delays. Moreover, the company's inventory management was inefficient, resulting in both excess stock and stockouts, which further strained its cash flow and customer relationships. Transportation costs were soaring due to poor route planning and an overreliance on air freight. The company needed to transform its supply chain to achieve greater efficiency, cost-effectiveness, and reliability.

The Strategy

To address these challenges, the company undertook a comprehensive supply chain transformation strategy focused on three key areas: supplier consolidation, advanced inventory management, and smart logistics.

1. **Supplier Consolidation and Collaboration**
   - It began by reducing its supplier base from 50 to 20, focusing on building stronger, more collaborative relationships with key suppliers. The company introduced a supplier scorecard system to evaluate performance based on quality, reliability, and cost-effectiveness. It also implemented long-term contracts with its top suppliers, incentivizing them to invest in capacity improvements and quality control measures.
   - **Example:** One key initiative was the development of a supplier development program, where it worked closely with its top five suppliers to improve their manufacturing processes. This included sharing best practices, providing technical support, and investing in joint research and development. The result was a 15% improvement in component quality and a 20% reduction in lead times.

2. **Advanced Inventory Management**
   - The company implemented an integrated inventory management system that provided real-time visibility across the entire supply chain. Using predictive analytics and machine learning, it forecasted demand more accurately, leading to better inventory planning and reducing the risk of stockouts and overstocking.

- **Example:** By adopting a just-in-time (JIT) inventory model, it was able to reduce its inventory levels by 30%, freeing up significant working capital. The predictive analytics tool helped the company anticipate demand spikes during peak seasons, ensuring that inventory was always at optimal levels. This resulted in a 25% reduction in stockouts and improved customer satisfaction ratings by 18%.

3. **Smart Logistics and Transportation Optimization**
   - To address the high transportation costs, the company invested in a transportation management system (TMS) that optimized routing and consolidated shipments. The TMS used AI to predict the most efficient routes, considering factors such as traffic patterns, weather conditions, and fuel costs. The company also diversified its transportation modes, shifting more shipments from air freight to sea and rail, which are more cost-effective.
   - **Example:** The company implemented a central logistics hub in Europe to serve its largest markets more efficiently. By consolidating shipments at this hub and then distributing them via regional carriers, it had cut its logistics costs by 20%. The optimized routing reduced delivery times by an average of three days, significantly improving customer service levels.

The Results

The company's overall supply chain costs were reduced by 25%, while delivery lead times were shortened by 30%. Inventory levels were optimized, leading to a 20% increase in cash flow and a 15% reduction in working capital requirements. Customer satisfaction soared, with on-time delivery rates improving from 85% to 98%.

Moreover, the stronger supplier relationships and improved logistics efficiency enabled it to introduce new products faster, capturing market share in competitive segments. The company's reputation for reliability and quality attracted new customers, leading to a 20% increase in sales within two years of the supply chain overhaul.

Conclusion

The company's successful supply chain implementation serves as a powerful example of how strategic changes in supplier management, inventory control, and logistics can transform a company's operations. By embracing technology, fostering collaboration with suppliers, and optimizing logistics, it turned its supply chain from a liability into a competitive advantage. This case study highlights the importance of a well-executed supply chain strategy in driving business growth and sustaining market leadership in a dynamic global environment.

Another example is of Nexa Tech. NexaTech, a rising star in the wearable technology sector, faced significant supply chain challenges that threatened its ambitious growth plans. Through strategic foresight, technological integration, and collaborative partnerships, NexaTech successfully re-engineered its supply chain, setting new benchmarks in the industry. This case study explores the innovative approaches NexaTech employed to achieve supply chain excellence and the lessons that other companies can draw from their experience.

CHAPTER 1   INTRODUCTION TO SUPPLY CHAIN MANAGEMENT

The Challenge

NexaTech, known for its cutting-edge smartwatches and fitness trackers, experienced rapid growth, leading to supply chain strains that jeopardized its ability to meet soaring customer demand. The company's reliance on a fragmented network of suppliers across Asia led to inconsistent product quality, unpredictable lead times, and escalating costs. Additionally, the absence of integrated inventory management and demand forecasting systems resulted in frequent stockouts and excess inventory, creating significant financial and operational challenges.

NexaTech's leadership recognized that to sustain its growth trajectory and maintain its competitive edge, it needed to transform its supply chain into a robust, agile, and responsive system capable of supporting global operations. The stakes were high, as any misstep could lead to lost market share and diminished brand reputation.

The Strategy

NexaTech embarked on a comprehensive supply chain transformation strategy with a focus on three core pillars: strategic supplier integration, advanced digitalization, and customer-centric logistics optimization.

1. **Strategic Supplier Integration**

    - NexaTech shifted from a transactional relationship model to a strategic partnership approach with key suppliers. The company reduced its supplier base by 40%, selecting partners based on their ability to provide high-quality components, scale with demand, and invest in joint innovation initiatives.

    - **Example:** NexaTech collaborated with a leading semiconductor manufacturer to co-develop custom chips for its next-generation smartwatches.

This partnership not only ensured a steady supply of critical components but also allowed for better alignment on production schedules and technological advancements, reducing lead times by 25% and improving product quality.

2. **Advanced Digitalization**

    - The cornerstone of NexaTech's supply chain overhaul was the implementation of a fully integrated digital platform that provided real-time visibility across the entire supply chain. This platform utilized artificial intelligence (AI) and machine learning (ML) to predict demand patterns, optimize inventory levels, and streamline procurement processes.

    - **Example:** NexaTech deployed an AI-driven demand forecasting tool that analyzed historical sales data, market trends, and external factors like seasonality and economic indicators. This tool enabled the company to achieve a 95% accuracy rate in its demand forecasts, significantly reducing the instances of stockouts and overproduction. The system also automated reordering processes, ensuring that inventory levels were always optimized, resulting in a 30% reduction in excess inventory.

3. **Customer-Centric Logistics Optimization**

    - To enhance its global distribution capabilities, NexaTech restructured its logistics network, focusing on creating regional distribution hubs closer to key markets. This move was supported by the adoption of a transportation management system (TMS) that optimized shipping routes, reduced transit times, and lowered transportation costs.

- **Example:** NexaTech established a central logistics hub in Europe, supported by smaller regional centers in North America and Asia. The TMS used real-time data to dynamically adjust shipping routes based on factors like traffic, weather conditions, and customs processing times. This approach not only reduced delivery times by an average of two days but also cut logistics costs by 15%, enhancing customer satisfaction and enabling faster response times to market changes.

The Results

The transformation of NexaTech's supply chain yielded impressive results, positioning the company as a leader in both operational efficiency and customer satisfaction. The integrated supplier partnerships led to a 20% reduction in component costs and a significant improvement in product quality, which in turn boosted customer trust and brand loyalty. The digitalization of the supply chain provided NexaTech with the agility to respond to market fluctuations swiftly, reducing lead times by 30% and cutting supply chain costs by 25%.

The logistics optimization strategy also paid off handsomely. The company's on-time delivery rate improved from 88% to 98%, and customer satisfaction scores increased by 15%. By reducing excess inventory and optimizing shipping routes, NexaTech freed up working capital, allowing the company to reinvest in R&D and marketing initiatives that further fueled its growth.

CHAPTER 1 INTRODUCTION TO SUPPLY CHAIN MANAGEMENT

NexaTech's supply chain transformation is a testament to the power of strategic foresight, technological innovation, and strong partnerships. By embracing a holistic approach to supply chain management, the company not only overcame its operational challenges but also turned its supply chain into a key competitive advantage. NexaTech's success story offers valuable insights for other companies looking to optimize their supply chains, particularly in how they can leverage digital tools, strategic supplier relationships, and customer-centric logistics to drive growth and efficiency in an increasingly complex global marketplace.

In conclusion, case studies of successful supply chain implementations, such as those of Zara, Amazon, Toyota, etc., demonstrate the practical applications and benefits of effective SCM. These examples highlight the importance of agility, efficiency, and technology in optimizing supply chain operations and achieving business success. By learning from these real-world examples, businesses can develop and implement strategies that enhance their own supply chain performance and drive competitive advantage.

CHAPTER 2
Production Planning and Control

Figure 2-1. Production Planning and Control

CHAPTER 2   PRODUCTION PLANNING AND CONTROL

Production planning and control (PPC) stands as the cornerstone of efficient manufacturing, ensuring that every aspect of production aligns seamlessly with business objectives and customer demands. In today's dynamic and competitive market, mastering PPC is not just advantageous—it's essential for survival and growth. This chapter explores the innovative methodologies and cutting-edge technologies that are redefining PPC, providing fresh insights and practical examples to illustrate its critical importance.

At its core, PPC encompasses the strategic planning, scheduling, and oversight of production activities to optimize resource utilization, minimize waste, and meet customer demands effectively. It involves a meticulous balancing act: forecasting future demand, allocating resources efficiently, and continuously monitoring production processes to ensure they run smoothly.

Traditional demand forecasting methods, which primarily relied on historical sales data and basic statistical models, often fell short in accuracy. Today, the integration of big data, machine learning, and artificial intelligence (AI) has revolutionized demand forecasting. These advanced technologies analyze vast amounts of data from various sources, including social media trends, consumer behavior patterns, and economic indicators, to provide more precise and actionable forecasts.

Production scheduling is a dynamic process that must adapt to real-time changes in demand, supply chain disruptions, and production bottlenecks. Advanced production scheduling systems now incorporate real-time data and analytics to create adaptive schedules that can respond to these fluctuations.

Examples from the previous chapter:

Consider a high-tech electronics company that produces smartphones. To meet the fluctuating market demand and rapid product evolution, this company employs advanced PPC strategies. It utilizes historical sales data, market trends, and predictive analytics to forecast demand accurately.

This allows it to plan production schedules and allocate resources, such as raw materials and labor, effectively. By doing so, it can meet customer demand promptly while avoiding overproduction and excess inventory costs.

A fashion retailer preparing for a new season can now leverage AI-driven demand forecasting. By analyzing data from social media platforms, online search trends, and historical sales, the AI model can predict which styles, colors, and sizes will be in demand. This enables the retailer to tailor its production plans accordingly, ensuring it has the right products in the right quantities to meet customer preferences.

2.1 Fundamentals of Production Planning

Production planning is the backbone of manufacturing operations, playing a critical role in ensuring that production processes run smoothly, efficiently, and cost-effectively. This foundational aspect of supply chain management involves forecasting demand, scheduling production activities, and strategically allocating resources. In this chapter, we will delve into the fundamentals of production planning, exploring innovative methods and providing fresh insights that illustrate its importance and application in modern manufacturing.

The Core of Production Planning

At its essence, production planning is about anticipating future production needs and devising a comprehensive plan to meet those needs. It encompasses several key activities:

1. **Resource Allocation**: Assigning the necessary resources, such as labor, materials, and machinery, to meet production goals

2. **Scheduling**: Creating a timeline for production activities to ensure that products are manufactured and delivered on time

Efficient Resource Allocation

Resource allocation is about ensuring that the right resources are available at the right time and place to meet production demands. This involves careful planning of materials, labor, and equipment. Effective resource allocation maximizes productivity and minimizes downtime.

Example: A pharmaceutical manufacturer producing a new drug must allocate resources efficiently to meet production targets. By using optimization algorithms, the manufacturer can determine the optimal number of workers needed for each shift, the required quantities of raw materials, and the best utilization of machinery. This ensures that the production process runs smoothly and that the drug is available for distribution on schedule.

Dynamic Production Scheduling

Production scheduling transforms the production plan into actionable timelines, detailing what will be produced, in what quantities, and by when. Modern production environments demand dynamic scheduling systems that can adapt to real-time changes in demand, supply chain disruptions, and production bottlenecks.

Example: A car manufacturer uses a dynamic scheduling system that integrates real-time data from its supply chain and production floor. If there is a delay in the delivery of a critical component, the system automatically adjusts the production schedule to prioritize other tasks. This minimizes downtime and ensures that the overall production plan remains on track.

2.2 Demand Forecasting Techniques

Demand forecasting is a critical component of production planning, enabling businesses to predict future customer demand and make informed decisions about inventory, production schedules, and resource allocation.

This process has evolved significantly with the advent of advanced technologies and sophisticated methodologies. In this section, we explore cutting-edge demand forecasting techniques that are transforming the way businesses anticipate and respond to market demand.

Leveraging Machine Learning for Demand Forecasting

Machine learning (ML) has revolutionized demand forecasting by enabling more accurate and dynamic predictions. Unlike traditional statistical methods, which rely heavily on historical data and fixed algorithms, ML models can analyze vast datasets, identify complex patterns, and adapt to changing conditions. These models continuously learn and improve over time, providing more precise forecasts.

Example: A global fashion retailer uses ML algorithms to forecast demand for its new seasonal collections. By analyzing data from previous seasons, current market trends, and even social media sentiment, the ML model predicts which styles, colors, and sizes will be popular. This allows the retailer to optimize its inventory and reduce the risk of stockouts or excess stock, thereby maximizing sales and minimizing waste.

Harnessing Big Data for Real-Time Insights

Big data has opened new avenues for demand forecasting by integrating diverse data sources and providing real-time insights. Companies can now aggregate data from various channels, including sales transactions, customer interactions, social media, and external factors like weather and economic indicators. This comprehensive approach offers a more holistic view of market demand.

Example: A supermarket chain employs big data analytics to forecast demand for perishable goods. By combining sales data with weather forecasts, local events, and social media trends, the chain can predict spikes in demand for items like ice cream during heatwaves or fresh produce during health trends. This real-time insight enables precise stock adjustments, reducing spoilage and ensuring fresh products for customers.

Predictive Analytics for Strategic Decision-Making

Predictive analytics combines statistical techniques, data mining, and machine learning to forecast future events. This approach is particularly useful for long-term demand forecasting, helping businesses make strategic decisions about product launches, market expansions, and resource investments. Predictive models consider a wide range of variables, including historical sales, market trends, and macroeconomic factors.

Example: An automotive manufacturer uses predictive analytics to forecast demand for electric vehicles (EVs) over the next decade. By analyzing trends in consumer preferences, government regulations, technological advancements, and competitive actions, the company can predict the growth trajectory of the EV market. This foresight informs strategic decisions about R&D investments, production capacity expansion, and marketing initiatives, positioning the company as a market leader.

The Role of Collaborative Forecasting

Collaborative forecasting involves sharing data and insights across the supply chain to improve forecast accuracy. By engaging suppliers, distributors, and retailers in the forecasting process, companies can gain a more comprehensive understanding of demand drivers and reduce information asymmetry. This approach fosters transparency and collaboration, leading to better-aligned production and inventory plans.

Example: A leading electronics manufacturer collaborates with its suppliers and major retailers to forecast demand for its latest gadgets. By sharing sales data, marketing plans, and market insights, all parties can contribute to a more accurate demand forecast. This collaborative effort ensures that suppliers are prepared with the necessary components, and retailers have sufficient stock to meet consumer demand during product launches.

Scenario Planning for Demand Uncertainty

Scenario planning is a technique used to forecast demand under different future scenarios, helping businesses prepare for uncertainty and volatility. By creating multiple scenarios based on various assumptions and potential events, companies can assess the impact of different factors on demand and develop contingency plans.

Example: A pharmaceutical company uses scenario planning to forecast demand for vaccines during a potential flu pandemic. By considering scenarios such as varying infection rates, government intervention levels, and public health responses, the company can estimate demand under different conditions. This preparation enables the company to adjust production plans, secure necessary resources, and ensure timely delivery of vaccines in the event of a pandemic.

2.3 Inventory Management

Inventory management is a pivotal aspect of supply chain operations, essential for maintaining the delicate balance between meeting customer demand and minimizing costs. Effective inventory management ensures that the right products are available at the right time, in the right quantities, while avoiding the pitfalls of overstocking or stockouts.

CHAPTER 2   PRODUCTION PLANNING AND CONTROL

This section explores innovative approaches to inventory management, offering fresh insights and practical examples to illustrate its significance and implementation in modern businesses.

The Essence of Inventory Management

At its core, inventory management involves overseeing the flow of goods from manufacturers to warehouses and finally to customers. This process includes tracking inventory levels, managing orders, and ensuring efficient storage and distribution. The primary goals are to optimize inventory levels, reduce carrying costs, and enhance customer satisfaction. Achieving these goals requires a strategic approach that integrates advanced technologies and data-driven decision-making.

Example: A major e-commerce platform utilizes sophisticated inventory management systems to handle the vast array of products it offers. By leveraging real-time data analytics, the platform can monitor inventory levels across multiple warehouses, predict demand trends, and adjust stock levels accordingly. This ensures that popular items are always in stock, while minimizing the risk of overstocking less popular products.

Just-in-Time (JIT) Inventory Management

Just-in-time (JIT) inventory management is a strategy that focuses on reducing inventory levels by receiving goods only as they are needed in the production process. This approach minimizes carrying costs and reduces waste but requires precise demand forecasting and a highly responsive supply chain.

Example: An automotive manufacturer implements JIT inventory management to streamline its production process. By working closely with suppliers, the manufacturer ensures that components arrive exactly when needed for assembly. This minimizes the storage space required for parts and reduces the costs associated with holding large inventories. However, JIT also demands a robust supply chain that can quickly adapt to changes in demand, avoiding potential delays.

Integrating Technology for Real-Time Inventory Tracking

The integration of technology in inventory management has brought about significant advancements in accuracy and efficiency. Technologies such as RFID (radio frequency identification), IoT (Internet of Things), and advanced analytics provide real-time visibility into inventory levels and movement.

Example: A fashion retailer uses RFID tags on all its products to track inventory in real time. These tags provide data on the exact location and status of each item, from the warehouse to the retail floor. This visibility enables the retailer to optimize stock levels, reduce shrinkage, and enhance the customer shopping experience by ensuring that products are readily available. Additionally, IoT sensors in the warehouse monitor environmental conditions to maintain the quality of sensitive items.

Demand-Driven Inventory Optimization

Demand-driven inventory optimization focuses on aligning inventory levels with the actual customer demand. This approach uses advanced analytics and machine learning algorithms to forecast demand accurately and adjust inventory levels dynamically.

Example: A consumer electronics company employs demand-driven inventory optimization to manage its diverse product range. By analyzing historical sales data, market trends, and customer preferences, the company can forecast demand for each product category. This enables them to adjust inventory levels proactively, ensuring that high-demand

31

items are sufficiently stocked, while reducing excess inventory of slower-moving products. This not only improves customer satisfaction but also enhances profitability by minimizing holding costs.

Sustainable Inventory Management Practices

Sustainability is becoming increasingly important in inventory management, as businesses strive to reduce their environmental impact. Sustainable practices involve minimizing waste, optimizing transportation, and adopting eco-friendly packaging and materials.

Example: A global food and beverage company adopts sustainable inventory management practices by implementing a circular supply chain. This involves reducing food waste through better demand forecasting and inventory rotation, using recyclable packaging, and optimizing transportation routes to reduce carbon emissions. By embracing sustainability, the company not only reduces its environmental footprint but also meets the growing consumer demand for eco-friendly products.

The Role of Automation in Inventory Management

Automation is transforming inventory management by streamlining processes and reducing the need for manual intervention. Automated systems can handle tasks such as inventory tracking, order processing, and replenishment, improving accuracy and efficiency.

Example: A large-scale warehouse employs automated guided vehicles (AGVs) and robotic systems to manage inventory. AGVs transport goods within the warehouse, while robots handle picking and packing tasks. This automation reduces the time and labor required for inventory management, increases accuracy, and allows the warehouse to operate 24/7. The integration of artificial intelligence further enhances these systems by optimizing routes and predicting maintenance needs.

2.4 Capacity Planning

Capacity planning is a strategic process that businesses use to ensure they have the right resources—such as equipment, labor, and facilities—at the right time to meet current and future production demands. This critical aspect of operations management involves forecasting future requirements, assessing existing capabilities, and making informed decisions to optimize capacity utilization. In this section, we explore the nuances of capacity planning, highlighting its importance, innovative approaches, and practical examples to illustrate its application in modern enterprises.

Understanding Capacity Planning

Capacity planning begins with a thorough assessment of current production capabilities and an analysis of anticipated future demands. By forecasting future requirements based on market trends, sales forecasts, and strategic objectives, businesses can determine their capacity needs over a specific time horizon. This proactive approach allows organizations to align their resources with expected demand, ensuring smooth operations and minimizing the risk of underutilization or overutilization of resources.

Example: A semiconductor manufacturer conducts capacity planning to prepare for the launch of a new generation of microchips. By analyzing market demand forecasts, technological advancements, and competitor activities, the manufacturer estimates the production capacity required to meet anticipated orders. This involves evaluating the capacity of production lines, assessing workforce capabilities, and ensuring that sufficient raw materials are available to support increased production volumes.

CHAPTER 2   PRODUCTION PLANNING AND CONTROL

Techniques for Effective Capacity Planning

Effective capacity planning employs various techniques to optimize resource allocation and enhance operational efficiency:

1. **Resource Forecasting:** Utilizing historical data, market trends, and predictive analytics to forecast future demand and align resources accordingly.

2. **Scenario Analysis:** Evaluating different scenarios and potential disruptions to anticipate capacity needs under varying conditions, such as market fluctuations or supply chain disruptions.

3. **Utilization Analysis:** Assessing the current utilization rates of production facilities, equipment, and labor to identify opportunities for optimization and efficiency improvements.

4. **Technology Integration:** Leveraging advanced technologies, such as simulation modeling and digital twin technology, to simulate production scenarios and optimize capacity allocation.

Example: An aerospace manufacturer integrates simulation modeling into its capacity planning process. By creating digital twins of production facilities and equipment, the manufacturer can simulate different production scenarios and assess the impact on capacity utilization. This allows them to identify potential bottlenecks, optimize production schedules, and make informed decisions about investments in additional capacity or equipment upgrades.

Strategic Investment in Capacity Expansion

Capacity planning also involves strategic decisions about capacity expansion or contraction based on long-term business goals and market dynamics. Businesses may invest in new facilities, upgrade existing infrastructure, or form strategic partnerships to enhance their production capabilities and meet growing demand effectively.

Example: A pharmaceutical company decides to expand its manufacturing capacity for a new vaccine. After conducting market research and evaluating regulatory requirements, the company invests in building a new state-of-the-art production facility. This strategic investment not only increases production capacity but also positions the company to capitalize on emerging market opportunities and maintain competitive advantage.

Balancing Flexibility and Efficiency

Achieving optimal capacity planning requires striking a balance between flexibility and efficiency. While businesses aim to maximize resource utilization and minimize costs, they must also remain agile and responsive to changes in market demand, technological advancements, and competitive pressures.

Example: A food processing company implements flexible manufacturing practices to accommodate seasonal fluctuations in demand for its products. By cross-training employees, adopting modular production systems, and maintaining strategic inventory buffers, the company can adjust production schedules and capacities dynamically. This flexibility enables them to meet customer demand promptly while minimizing excess capacity during off-peak seasons.

Continuous Improvement Through Data-Driven Insights

Capacity planning is an iterative process that relies on continuous improvement and data-driven insights. By analyzing performance metrics, conducting postmortem reviews of production cycles, and soliciting feedback from stakeholders, businesses can refine their capacity planning strategies and optimize resource allocation over time.

Example: A global automotive manufacturer uses performance analytics and stakeholder feedback to continuously improve its capacity planning processes. By identifying inefficiencies, optimizing production schedules, and investing in employee training, the manufacturer enhances productivity, reduces lead times, and improves overall operational performance.

2.5 Production Scheduling and Control

Production scheduling and control are integral to the smooth operation of manufacturing processes, ensuring that production activities are planned, coordinated, and executed efficiently. This part explores the intricacies of production scheduling and control, highlighting its significance, innovative approaches, and practical examples to illustrate its application in modern manufacturing environments.

The Essence of Production Scheduling

Production scheduling involves creating a timeline or roadmap that dictates when and where specific tasks or operations will be performed within the production process. It encompasses assigning resources, setting timelines, and coordinating activities to maximize efficiency and meet production goals. Effective scheduling ensures that manufacturing processes run smoothly, products are delivered on time, and resources are utilized optimally.

Example: A high-tech electronics manufacturer uses advanced scheduling software to plan production for its latest smartphone model. The software considers factors such as production capacity, resource availability, and order priorities to create an optimized schedule. This ensures that each production stage—from component assembly to quality control—is completed efficiently, minimizing downtime and accelerating time-to-market.

Strategies for Effective Production Scheduling

Effective production scheduling employs several strategies to streamline operations and enhance productivity:

1. **Finite Capacity Scheduling:** Optimizing production schedules based on the finite capacity of resources, such as machinery, labor, and materials, to prevent bottlenecks and maximize throughput.

2. **Just-in-Time (JIT) Scheduling:** Aligning production schedules with customer demand by scheduling tasks and orders to minimize inventory-holding costs and reduce lead times.

3. **Sequencing and Prioritization:** Determining the order in which tasks or orders are processed to prioritize urgent or high-priority items and ensure timely delivery.

4. **Resource Optimization:** Balancing workload across machines, workstations, and shifts to maximize resource utilization and minimize idle time.

Example: An automotive assembly plant implements finite capacity scheduling to optimize its production line. By analyzing machine capacities, labor availability, and production sequences, the plant schedules vehicle assembly in a way that maximizes efficiency and minimizes production delays. This approach allows the plant to meet fluctuating demand while maintaining high standards of quality and efficiency.

Real-Time Monitoring and Control

Production control involves monitoring ongoing production activities in real time, making adjustments as needed to ensure adherence to the schedule and quality standards. This proactive approach enables manufacturers to respond promptly to disruptions, optimize resource allocation, and maintain consistency in production output.

Example: A pharmaceutical company uses real-time monitoring systems in its production facilities to control the manufacturing process of medicines. Sensors and automated systems track parameters such as temperature, pressure, and chemical composition during each production batch. If deviations are detected, the system alerts operators who can take corrective action immediately, ensuring compliance with regulatory requirements and product quality standards.

Lean Manufacturing Principles in Production Scheduling

Lean manufacturing principles advocate for minimizing waste and maximizing value-added activities throughout the production process. Applying lean principles to production scheduling involves eliminating bottlenecks, reducing setup times, and implementing pull-based systems to synchronize production with customer demand.

Example: A lean-focused electronics manufacturer employs Kanban systems in production scheduling. Kanban cards signal when and how much of each component is needed based on customer demand. This just-in-time approach minimizes inventory storage costs and ensures that production flows smoothly without overproduction or excess inventory.

Integration of Advanced Technologies

The integration of advanced technologies, such as artificial intelligence (AI), Internet of Things (IoT), and big data analytics, is transforming production scheduling and control. These technologies provide predictive insights, automate decision-making processes, and optimize production schedules in real time.

Example: A food processing company utilizes AI-powered predictive analytics to optimize production scheduling for its perishable products. By analyzing historical sales data, market demand forecasts, and supply chain dynamics, the AI system generates production schedules that minimize waste and maximize freshness. IoT sensors monitor production conditions, ensuring compliance with food safety standards and optimizing resource utilization.

Continuous Improvement and Adaptability

Continuous improvement is essential in production scheduling and control, as businesses strive to enhance efficiency, reduce costs, and adapt to changing market conditions. By conducting performance reviews, gathering feedback from stakeholders, and leveraging data analytics, manufacturers can refine their scheduling strategies and achieve operational excellence.

Example: A consumer goods manufacturer conducts regular performance reviews of its production scheduling processes. By analyzing key performance indicators (KPIs) such as on-time delivery rates, production cycle times, and resource utilization metrics, the manufacturer identifies areas for improvement. This continuous improvement approach allows it to implement corrective actions, optimize production schedules, and maintain competitiveness in the market.

2.6 Lean Manufacturing Principles

Lean manufacturing principles represent a systematic approach to eliminating waste, optimizing processes, and maximizing value across the entire production chain. Originating from the Toyota Production System (TPS), these principles have revolutionized manufacturing by focusing on continuous improvement, respect for people, and delivering products with the highest quality and efficiency. In this section, we delve into the core principles of lean manufacturing, illustrating their application, benefits, and real-world examples to highlight their transformative impact on modern manufacturing practices.

Elimination of Waste: The Foundation of Lean

At the heart of lean manufacturing is the relentless pursuit of waste reduction across all aspects of production. Waste, in lean terms, refers to any activity or resource that does not add value to the final product. By identifying and eliminating waste, manufacturers can streamline operations, reduce costs, and improve overall efficiency.

Example: A furniture manufacturer adopts lean principles to minimize waste in its production processes. Through value stream mapping and Kaizen events, the manufacturer identifies inefficiencies such as overproduction, excess inventory, and unnecessary motion in the production line. By eliminating these wastes, the manufacturer reduces lead times, improves product quality, and enhances customer satisfaction.

CHAPTER 2   PRODUCTION PLANNING AND CONTROL

Continuous Improvement (Kaizen)

Figure 2-2. Importance of Planning and Action in Continuous Improvement

Kaizen, or continuous improvement, is a fundamental aspect of lean manufacturing that encourages all employees—from frontline workers to senior management—to seek incremental improvements in processes, products, and workflows. This philosophy fosters a culture of innovation, collaboration, and problem-solving, driving sustainable improvements over time.

Example: An automotive assembly plant implements Kaizen principles to optimize its production line. Employees are empowered to suggest and implement small-scale improvements, such as rearranging workstations for better workflow, standardizing tools and procedures, and reducing setup times. These continuous improvements result in higher productivity, lower costs, and greater employee satisfaction.

CHAPTER 2   PRODUCTION PLANNING AND CONTROL

Respect for People

Lean manufacturing places a strong emphasis on respecting and empowering people within the organization. By valuing the expertise and contributions of employees, organizations can harness their full potential to drive innovation, improve processes, and achieve shared goals.

Example: A medical device manufacturer embraces lean principles by involving frontline workers in decision-making processes. Teams participate in daily huddles to discuss challenges, share insights, and propose solutions. This collaborative approach not only enhances communication and teamwork but also leads to faster problem resolution and better outcomes for patients.

Pull Production Systems

Lean manufacturing promotes the use of pull production systems, where production is driven by actual customer demand rather than forecasted estimates. This approach minimizes inventory holding costs, reduces lead times, and ensures that production aligns closely with market demand fluctuations.

Example: An electronics manufacturer implements a Kanban system to facilitate pull production. Kanban cards signal the need for replenishment based on real-time customer orders. This enables the manufacturer to produce goods in response to actual demand, maintain optimal inventory levels, and improve cash flow by reducing excess inventory.

Value Stream Mapping

Value stream mapping is a tool used in lean manufacturing to visualize and analyze the flow of materials and information required to bring a product from raw material to customer delivery. By identifying value-adding and non-value-adding activities, organizations can streamline processes, reduce cycle times, and enhance overall efficiency.

Example: A pharmaceutical company uses value stream mapping to optimize its drug manufacturing process. By mapping the flow of materials, information, and personnel from raw material procurement to final product distribution, the company identifies bottlenecks, redundancies, and opportunities for improvement. This strategic approach helps it streamline operations, reduce waste, and deliver medications to market faster.

CHAPTER 3

Logistics and Distribution Management

Figure 3-1. *Logistics and Distribution Management*

CHAPTER 3 LOGISTICS AND DISTRIBUTION MANAGEMENT

Logistics and distribution management are the unsung heroes of the modern economy, quietly powering the global trade system that delivers goods from manufacturers to consumers. These processes encompass the planning, implementation, and control of the movement and storage of goods, services, and information within a supply chain. They ensure that products reach the right place, at the right time, in the right quantity, and at the right cost. As global markets continue to expand and customer expectations evolve, efficient logistics and distribution have become critical to maintaining competitiveness and ensuring customer satisfaction.

At its core, logistics management involves coordinating and optimizing various activities, such as transportation, warehousing, inventory management, packaging, and order fulfillment. These activities must be seamlessly integrated to create a smooth and cost-effective flow of goods from the point of origin to the point of consumption. In today's world, where supply chains are increasingly complex and geographically dispersed, the role of logistics has expanded beyond mere transportation. It now includes managing risks, ensuring compliance with international regulations, and leveraging technology to enhance visibility and efficiency.

One of the most significant challenges in logistics management is balancing cost and service quality. Companies must ensure that their logistics operations are cost-effective while still meeting customer demands for speed, reliability, and flexibility. This balancing act often involves making strategic decisions about transportation modes, warehouse locations, and inventory levels. For instance, a company may choose to use air freight for high-value, time-sensitive products, despite the higher cost, to meet tight delivery deadlines. Conversely, for bulk shipments that are less time-sensitive, ocean freight may be a more cost-effective option.

Distribution management, a subset of logistics, focuses specifically on the movement of finished goods from the end of the production line to the end customer. This process includes selecting distribution channels, managing relationships with distributors and retailers, and optimizing

CHAPTER 3   LOGISTICS AND DISTRIBUTION MANAGEMENT

the distribution network to minimize costs and delivery times. The rise of e-commerce has dramatically altered the distribution landscape, as companies now need to fulfill orders directly to consumers, often within tight time frames. This shift has led to the development of sophisticated distribution strategies, such as omnichannel fulfillment, where orders can be fulfilled from a combination of warehouses, stores, and third-party logistics providers.

One of the most transformative developments in logistics and distribution management in recent years has been the integration of advanced technologies. The adoption of digital tools such as artificial intelligence (AI), machine learning (ML), and the Internet of Things (IoT) has revolutionized the way companies manage their supply chains. For example, AI-driven analytics can optimize routing decisions in real time, reducing transportation costs and improving delivery times. IoT devices can track shipments throughout the supply chain, providing real-time visibility and enabling companies to respond quickly to disruptions. Moreover, blockchain technology is being explored for its potential to enhance transparency and traceability in the supply chain, reducing the risk of fraud and ensuring the authenticity of products.

Sustainability is another critical consideration in modern logistics and distribution management. As environmental concerns grow, companies are under increasing pressure to reduce their carbon footprint and adopt more sustainable practices. This has led to the development of green logistics strategies, such as optimizing transportation routes to reduce fuel consumption, using eco-friendly packaging materials, and adopting energy-efficient technologies in warehouses.

This chapter talks about how logistics and distribution management are essential components of a successful supply chain, directly impacting a company's bottom line and customer satisfaction. As global trade continues to evolve, the ability to effectively manage these processes will be a key determinant of competitive advantage. Companies that invest

CHAPTER 3   LOGISTICS AND DISTRIBUTION MANAGEMENT

in advanced technologies, embrace sustainability, and develop agile and responsive logistics and distribution networks will be well-positioned to thrive in the future.

3.1 Overview of Logistics Management

Logistics management is the heart of any supply chain, acting as the critical link between the production of goods and their final delivery to the customer. It encompasses a wide range of activities, from transportation and warehousing to inventory control and order fulfillment. In today's increasingly globalized and complex market environment, logistics management is not just about moving products from point A to point B. It is about optimizing the entire process to ensure that goods are delivered in the most efficient, cost-effective, and customer-friendly manner possible.

The Role and Importance of Logistics Management

At its core, logistics management involves the detailed planning, execution, and control of the flow of goods, services, and information within a supply chain. The primary goal is to ensure that the right product reaches the right customer, at the right time, and in the right condition. This requires careful coordination of multiple functions, including transportation, warehousing, inventory management, packaging, and order processing.

In the modern business landscape, logistics management has evolved from being a purely operational function to a strategic one. Companies now recognize that effective logistics can provide a significant competitive advantage, enabling them to respond quickly to market changes, reduce operational costs, and enhance customer satisfaction. For instance, companies like Amazon and Walmart have built their success on the foundation of highly efficient logistics and distribution networks, allowing them to offer fast, reliable, and cost-effective delivery services that meet the ever-growing expectations of consumers.

Key Components of Logistics Management

1. **Transportation Management**

   Transportation is the most visible and arguably the most critical component of logistics management. It involves the physical movement of goods from one location to another, whether by road, rail, air, or sea. Effective transportation management requires selecting the appropriate mode of transport based on factors such as cost, speed, distance, and the nature of the goods being transported.

   For example, a company shipping perishable goods like fresh produce or pharmaceuticals must prioritize speed and reliability, often opting for air freight despite its higher cost. Conversely, a company moving large volumes of nonperishable goods, such as electronics or clothing, may choose ocean freight for its cost-effectiveness, even though it takes longer.

   A real-life example of innovative transportation management is found in the operations of FedEx. The company's hub-and-spoke model allows it to consolidate shipments at central hubs before dispatching them to their final destinations. This model has enabled FedEx to offer overnight delivery services on a global scale, setting a benchmark for speed and reliability in the logistics industry.

2. **Warehousing and Inventory Management**

   Warehousing involves the storage of goods until they are needed for production or delivery to customers. Effective warehousing strategies are essential for maintaining the flow of goods within a supply chain, ensuring that products are readily available when and where they are needed.

   Inventory management is closely linked to warehousing and involves tracking the quantity, location, and condition of stock at any given time. The goal is to maintain optimal inventory levels—enough to meet customer demand without tying up excessive capital in stock that may become obsolete or damaged.

3. **Order Fulfillment**

   Order fulfillment is the process of receiving, processing, and delivering customer orders. It involves several steps, including order entry, picking and packing, and shipping. Efficient order fulfillment is crucial for meeting customer expectations and building brand loyalty.

4. **Demand Forecasting and Planning**

   Accurate demand forecasting is essential for logistics management, as it helps companies anticipate customer demand and plan their logistics activities accordingly. Demand forecasting involves analyzing historical sales data, market trends, and external factors such as seasonality and economic conditions to predict future demand.

A real-life example of effective demand forecasting can be seen in the operations of Procter & Gamble (P&G). P&G uses advanced data analytics and machine learning algorithms to forecast demand for its wide range of consumer products. These forecasts inform the company's production and distribution plans, helping it to avoid stockouts and overproduction. By aligning its logistics activities with demand forecasts, P&G can reduce costs, improve customer service, and enhance overall supply chain efficiency.

5. **Customer Service and Reverse Logistics**

Customer service is a critical aspect of logistics management, as it directly impacts customer satisfaction and loyalty. This involves ensuring that orders are delivered accurately and on time, handling customer inquiries and complaints, and managing returns and exchanges.

Reverse logistics, the process of handling returned goods, is becoming increasingly important as more companies adopt e-commerce and direct-to-consumer models. Effective reverse logistics can help companies recover value from returned products, reduce waste, and improve customer satisfaction.

For example, the online fashion retailer ASOS a customer of DHL has developed a highly efficient reverse logistics system to manage the high volume of returns it receives from customers. ASOS uses a combination of automated returns processing and data analytics to quickly assess the condition of returned items, determine whether they can be resold, and process refunds. This system enables ASOS to maintain a high level of customer satisfaction while minimizing the cost and environmental impact of returns.

The Impact of Technology on Logistics Management

The integration of advanced technologies into logistics management has transformed the industry, enabling companies to achieve greater efficiency, visibility, and agility. Some of the key technological innovations shaping the future of logistics include

1. **Internet of Things (IoT):** IoT devices, such as GPS trackers and RFID tags, provide real-time visibility into the location and condition of goods as they move through the supply chain. This allows companies to monitor shipments, track inventory levels, and respond quickly to disruptions.

2. **Artificial Intelligence (AI) and Machine Learning (ML):** AI and ML algorithms can analyze vast amounts of data to optimize logistics activities, such as demand forecasting, route planning, and inventory management. These technologies enable companies to make more informed decisions, reduce costs, and improve customer service.

3. **Blockchain:** Blockchain technology is being explored for its potential to enhance transparency and traceability in the supply chain. By creating a secure, tamper-proof record of transactions,

blockchain can help companies verify the authenticity of products, prevent fraud, and ensure compliance with regulations.

4. **Automation and Robotics:** Automation and robotics are transforming warehousing and order fulfillment operations. Automated systems can handle repetitive tasks, such as picking and packing, more quickly and accurately than humans, reducing labor costs and improving efficiency.

3.2 Transportation Management

Transportation management is a critical component of supply chain logistics, encompassing the planning, execution, and optimization of the movement of goods. Whether goods are moving from manufacturers to distribution centers, from suppliers to factories, or directly to end customers, transportation management ensures that these movements are efficient, cost-effective, and aligned with customer expectations. In the context of globalization and e-commerce, where speed, reliability, and flexibility are paramount, mastering transportation management is more important than ever.

The Strategic Importance of Transportation Management

Transportation is not just about moving goods from one place to another; it's about doing so in a way that aligns with broader business objectives. Transportation costs typically represent a significant portion of total logistics expenses, often exceeding 50% in many industries. As such, transportation management directly impacts a company's bottom line.

Efficient transportation strategies can reduce costs, enhance delivery speed, and improve customer satisfaction—three critical factors in today's competitive marketplace.

Moreover, transportation management is a key enabler of supply chain agility. In an era where customer expectations for rapid delivery are high, and supply chain disruptions are increasingly common, the ability to quickly adjust transportation plans is a significant competitive advantage. Companies that can reroute shipments, shift between different modes of transport, and respond swiftly to unexpected changes are better positioned to meet customer demands and minimize the impact of disruptions.

Key Components of Transportation Management

1. **Transportation Planning**

    Effective transportation management begins with careful planning. This involves selecting the most appropriate transportation modes (e.g., road, rail, air, sea) based on factors such as cost, speed, distance, and the nature of the goods being transported. Transportation planning also involves route optimization, which is the process of determining the most efficient path for goods to travel. Route optimization considers variables such as distance, traffic patterns, fuel costs, tolls, and environmental impact. For example, UPS uses advanced algorithms to minimize left turns on delivery routes, reducing idling time, fuel consumption, and emissions.

CHAPTER 3   LOGISTICS AND DISTRIBUTION MANAGEMENT

2. **Carrier Selection and Management**

   Selecting the right carriers—whether trucking companies, rail operators, or ocean freight liners—is another crucial aspect of transportation management. Companies must evaluate carriers based on reliability, cost, capacity, and service levels. Building strong relationships with carriers can lead to better service, more favorable rates, and priority access to capacity during peak seasons.

   Carrier management also involves negotiating contracts, monitoring carrier performance, and ensuring compliance with regulations. For example, a company might use a combination of regional carriers for short-haul deliveries and national carriers for long-haul routes, depending on the geographic distribution of its customers and suppliers. Technology plays a significant role here, with transportation management systems (TMS) offering tools to track carrier performance, manage contracts, and facilitate communication between shippers and carriers.

3. **Freight Consolidation and Load Optimization**

   Freight consolidation is the practice of combining multiple shipments into a single load to maximize the utilization of transportation assets. This is particularly important for companies with smaller, less-than-truckload (LTL) shipments, as consolidating these into full truckloads (FTL) can significantly reduce transportation costs.

Load optimization goes hand-in-hand with freight consolidation. It involves arranging the goods within a truck, container, or other transport unit in a way that maximizes space utilization while ensuring the safety and integrity of the cargo. For instance, a company shipping a mix of heavy and fragile items might strategically place the heavier items at the bottom and lighter, more delicate items on top to prevent damage.

An innovative example of freight consolidation and load optimization can be seen in the operations of Amazon. The company uses sophisticated algorithms to determine the most efficient way to pack its delivery vehicles, taking into account factors like package size, weight, and destination. This not only reduces transportation costs but also enables Amazon to offer fast and reliable delivery services.

4. **Real-Time Tracking and Visibility**

In today's digital age, real-time tracking and visibility are essential for effective transportation management. Customers and businesses alike expect to know the exact location of their shipments at any given time. This transparency not only builds trust but also allows companies to proactively manage any issues that may arise during transit.

Real-time tracking is made possible through the use of GPS technology, IoT devices, and advanced tracking software. For example, companies like DHL and FedEx offer customers the ability to track their shipments in real time via mobile apps and online portals. These platforms provide updates on the location of the shipment, estimated delivery times, and any delays or issues encountered along the way.

Beyond customer-facing applications, real-time visibility also plays a critical role in internal operations. Transportation managers can use this data to monitor the performance of their carriers, optimize routes, and quickly respond to disruptions, such as road closures or adverse weather conditions. By having a clear view of where goods are at all times, companies can make more informed decisions and improve the overall efficiency of their transportation networks.

5. **Sustainability in Transportation Management**

   As environmental concerns grow, sustainability has become a key consideration in transportation management. Companies are under increasing pressure to reduce their carbon footprint and adopt greener practices in their logistics operations. This can involve a range of strategies, from optimizing routes to reduce fuel consumption to investing in electric or hybrid vehicles.

   A leading example of sustainable transportation management is the approach taken by Unilever. The company has committed to reducing its logistics-related CO_2 emissions by using more fuel-efficient vehicles, optimizing routes, and increasing the use of rail transport, which has a lower environmental impact compared to road transport. Additionally, Unilever is exploring the use of biofuels and other alternative energy sources to further reduce its environmental footprint.

Another innovative approach to sustainability is the concept of "collaborative logistics," where companies share transportation resources to reduce empty miles and improve load efficiency. For instance, several European companies have formed logistics partnerships to share truck space, reducing the number of vehicles on the road and lowering emissions.

The Role of Technology in Transportation Management

Technology is revolutionizing transportation management, offering new tools and capabilities to improve efficiency, reduce costs, and enhance customer satisfaction. Some of the most impactful technologies include:

1. **Transportation Management Systems (TMS):** TMS platforms provide a centralized hub for managing all aspects of transportation, from planning and execution to monitoring and optimization. These systems enable companies to automate key processes, such as route planning and carrier selection, while providing real-time insights into transportation performance.

2. **Big Data and Analytics:** The vast amounts of data generated by transportation operations can be harnessed to drive smarter decision-making. Advanced analytics can identify patterns and trends, predict demand, optimize routes, and improve carrier performance.

3. **Autonomous Vehicles and Drones:** While still in the early stages of adoption, autonomous vehicles and drones have the potential to transform transportation management. These technologies could significantly reduce labor costs, increase delivery speed, and improve safety. For example, companies like UPS and Amazon are experimenting with drone deliveries for last-mile logistics, offering the potential for faster and more flexible delivery options.

4. **Blockchain:** Blockchain technology offers a secure and transparent way to track goods throughout the supply chain. By creating an immutable record of every transaction, blockchain can help prevent fraud, ensure the authenticity of goods, and improve the traceability of shipments.

CHAPTER 3   LOGISTICS AND DISTRIBUTION MANAGEMENT

3.3 Warehousing and Storage Solutions

Figure 3-2. Warehousing and Storage Solutions

Warehousing and storage solutions are foundational elements of any effective supply chain, serving as critical nodes that enable the efficient flow of goods from producers to consumers. As global commerce has evolved, so too have the demands on warehousing, requiring sophisticated systems and technologies to manage the increasing complexity and scale of modern supply chains. This chapter delves into the intricacies of warehousing and storage solutions, exploring how they contribute to overall supply chain efficiency, the latest innovations in the field, and real-world examples of companies that have leveraged these solutions to gain a competitive edge.

CHAPTER 3   LOGISTICS AND DISTRIBUTION MANAGEMENT

The Role of Warehousing in the Supply Chain

At its core, a warehouse is more than just a space to store goods; it is a strategic asset that supports various supply chain functions, including inventory management, order fulfillment, and distribution. The primary purpose of warehousing is to provide a buffer between the production and consumption of goods, ensuring that products are available when and where they are needed.

Warehouses also play a crucial role in managing the variability of supply and demand. For instance, in industries with seasonal demand, such as retail or agriculture, warehouses enable companies to stockpile products during periods of low demand and release them during peak seasons. This capability helps stabilize supply chains, reduce lead times, and improve customer satisfaction by ensuring product availability.

Moreover, warehousing supports value-added services such as packaging, labeling, and product customization. These services allow companies to tailor products to specific customer needs or regional markets, enhancing their ability to compete in a globalized economy. For example, a global electronics manufacturer might use a warehouse to configure products with region-specific power adapters or software before shipping them to different markets.

Types of Warehousing Solutions

The world of warehousing is diverse, with different types of warehouses serving various needs within the supply chain. Understanding these distinctions is crucial for selecting the right warehousing solution for a business.

1. **Public Warehouses:** These are third-party facilities that offer storage space on a rental basis. Public warehouses are ideal for companies that require

flexible storage solutions, as they allow businesses to scale their storage capacity up or down based on demand. For instance, a small e-commerce retailer might use a public warehouse during the holiday season to handle increased inventory, avoiding the costs associated with owning and maintaining a dedicated facility.

2. **Private Warehouses:** Owned and operated by the company using them, private warehouses offer greater control over operations and are often used by businesses with stable, high-volume storage needs. Companies with complex supply chains, such as large retailers or manufacturers, often invest in private warehouses to ensure that their specific requirements for layout, equipment, and technology are met.

3. **Automated Warehouses:** These facilities leverage advanced technology, such as robotics and automated storage and retrieval systems (AS/RS), to optimize storage density and throughput. Automated warehouses are particularly valuable in environments where speed and accuracy are critical, such as in the fulfillment of online orders.

4. **Climate-Controlled Warehouses:** Certain products, such as pharmaceuticals, food, and electronics, require specific environmental conditions to maintain their quality. Climate-controlled warehouses offer temperature and humidity regulation, ensuring that sensitive products remain in optimal condition. For example, a pharmaceutical

company might use a climate-controlled warehouse to store vaccines, which require consistent low temperatures to remain effective.

5. **Distribution Centers:** Unlike traditional warehouses, which primarily store goods, distribution centers are designed for the rapid movement of products. These facilities are strategically located close to major markets or transportation hubs to minimize delivery times.

Innovations in Warehousing: The Future of Storage Solutions

The landscape of warehousing is rapidly evolving, driven by advancements in technology and the growing complexity of global supply chains. Several key innovations are transforming the way companies manage their warehousing and storage needs.

1. **Artificial Intelligence (AI) and Machine Learning:** AI is increasingly being used to optimize warehouse operations, from demand forecasting to inventory management. Machine learning algorithms can analyze vast amounts of data to predict trends, such as which products will be in high demand in the coming months, enabling warehouses to adjust their inventory levels accordingly. For example, Walmart uses AI to manage its inventory and anticipate restocking needs, reducing stockouts and excess inventory.

2. **Internet of Things (IoT):** IoT devices are being deployed throughout warehouses to provide real-time visibility into operations. Sensors can track

the movement of goods, monitor environmental conditions, and even alert managers to potential issues, such as equipment failures or temperature fluctuations. A logistics company might use IoT-enabled sensors to monitor the temperature of perishable goods in transit, ensuring that they arrive in perfect condition.

3. **Blockchain Technology:** Blockchain is being explored as a tool for enhancing transparency and security in warehousing operations. By providing a decentralized, tamper-proof record of transactions, blockchain can help verify the authenticity of goods, track their movement through the supply chain, and reduce the risk of fraud. For instance, a luxury goods manufacturer could use blockchain to track the provenance of its products, ensuring that only genuine items reach consumers.

4. **Sustainable Warehousing:** As environmental concerns become more pressing, companies are increasingly focusing on sustainable warehousing practices. This includes the use of energy-efficient lighting, renewable energy sources, and eco-friendly building materials. Additionally, some companies are adopting green logistics practices, such as optimizing transportation routes to reduce carbon emissions. An example of this is IKEA, which has committed to using 100% renewable energy in its warehouses and is working toward making its supply chain climate-positive by 2030.

5. **3D Printing:** While still emerging, 3D printing has the potential to revolutionize warehousing by enabling on-demand manufacturing of parts and products. This could drastically reduce the need for large inventories, as items could be produced as needed, closer to the point of consumption. A company like Airbus, for instance, might use 3D printing to produce aircraft parts on demand, reducing the need for extensive storage facilities and speeding up the repair process.

Real-World Applications: Success Stories in Warehousing

Several companies have successfully implemented innovative warehousing solutions to enhance their supply chain efficiency. One such example is Alibaba, the Chinese e-commerce giant. Alibaba's logistics arm, Cainiao, has developed highly automated warehouses that use robotics, AI, and big data to manage the fulfillment of millions of orders daily. These warehouses are capable of processing orders with incredible speed and accuracy, supporting Alibaba's goal of delivering packages anywhere in China within 24 hours.

Another example is Tesla, which has revolutionized automotive warehousing by integrating it closely with production. Tesla's gigafactories are designed to minimize the distance between warehousing and manufacturing, allowing for just-in-time inventory management and reducing the need for extensive storage facilities. This approach has enabled Tesla to scale its production rapidly while maintaining high levels of efficiency and cost-effectiveness.

As supply chains become more complex and customer expectations continue to rise, the role of warehousing will only grow in importance. By embracing new technologies and innovative practices, companies can transform their warehousing operations into strategic assets that drive competitive advantage and support long-term success. Whether through automation, sustainability initiatives, or advanced data analytics, the future of warehousing promises to be dynamic, efficient, and integral to the supply chains of tomorrow.

3.4 Distribution Network Design

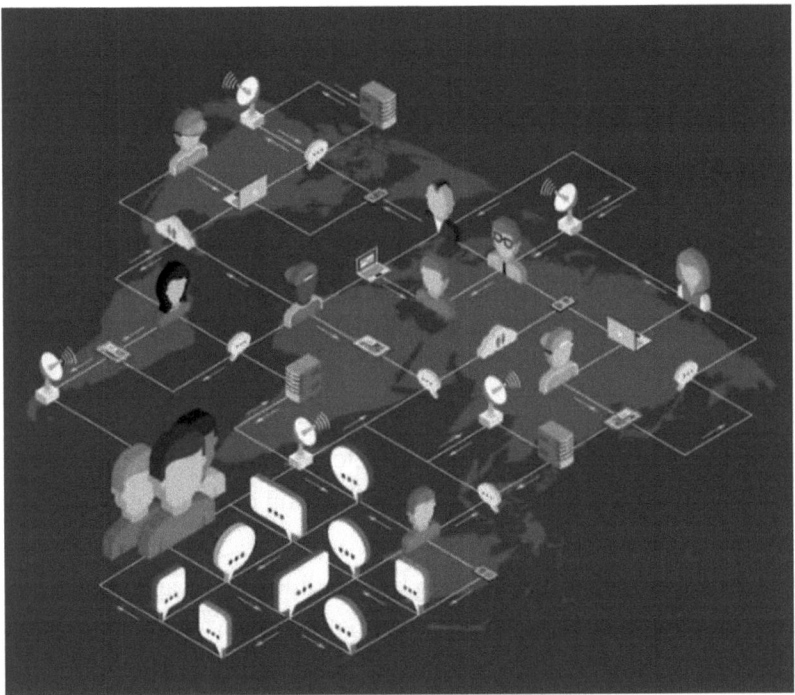

Figure 3-3. Distribution Network Design (Source: Global Internet Forum)

Distribution network design is a critical element in the architecture of any successful supply chain. It encompasses the strategic planning and arrangement of facilities, transportation routes, and inventory locations that enable the efficient movement of goods from producers to consumers. As global markets become increasingly interconnected, the complexity of designing an optimal distribution network grows, requiring businesses to balance cost, service levels, and flexibility in a highly competitive environment.

In this chapter, we will explore the intricacies of distribution network design, examining the factors that influence its configuration, the methodologies employed to develop it, and the impact of emerging technologies. Real-world examples will illustrate how companies have successfully designed and adapted their distribution networks to meet evolving market demands.

The Strategic Importance of Distribution Network Design

At its core, distribution network design determines how efficiently a company can serve its customers while managing costs and maintaining service quality. An effective distribution network minimizes the total cost of ownership by optimizing the location and size of facilities, inventory levels, and transportation routes. This not only reduces operational expenses but also enhances the company's ability to respond to market changes, such as shifts in consumer demand or disruptions in supply chains.

For example, a global consumer goods company might choose to establish regional distribution centers (DCs) closer to key markets. This strategy reduces transportation costs and lead times, allowing the company to quickly restock retail locations and meet customer demand. Conversely, a company with a less optimal distribution network might face higher costs, longer delivery times, and greater difficulty in managing inventory across multiple locations.

CHAPTER 3   LOGISTICS AND DISTRIBUTION MANAGEMENT

Key Factors Influencing Distribution Network Design

Designing a distribution network involves a complex interplay of factors, each of which must be carefully considered to create a network that is both efficient and adaptable. Some of the most critical factors include:

1. **Customer Demand:** Understanding the geographic distribution of customer demand is fundamental to network design. Companies must analyze where their customers are located, the frequency and volume of their orders, and the required service levels. For instance, a company that serves a dense urban market may prioritize proximity to customers, while a company with a more dispersed customer base may focus on optimizing transportation routes.

2. **Cost Considerations:** Cost is a driving factor in network design. This includes the cost of facilities (such as warehouses and distribution centers), transportation, inventory, and labor. Companies must balance these costs against the need to maintain service levels. For example, a company might decide to consolidate its warehousing operations into fewer, larger facilities to achieve economies of scale, even if this results in longer transportation routes.

3. **Service Levels:** The level of service that a company provides to its customers—such as delivery speed, order accuracy, and availability—directly impacts customer satisfaction and loyalty. Distribution network design must align with the company's service goals. A retailer offering same-day

CHAPTER 3   LOGISTICS AND DISTRIBUTION MANAGEMENT

delivery, for instance, requires a highly responsive distribution network with strategically located fulfillment centers near major metropolitan areas.

4. **Supply Chain Resilience:** In today's volatile global economy, supply chain resilience has become a crucial consideration. Companies must design networks that can withstand disruptions, such as natural disasters, political instability, or supply shortages. This might involve diversifying suppliers, adding redundancy in critical locations, or creating contingency plans for rapid reconfiguration of the network.

5. **Sustainability:** As sustainability becomes a key focus for businesses and consumers alike, distribution network design increasingly incorporates environmental considerations. Companies are exploring ways to reduce carbon emissions, such as optimizing transportation routes, using energy-efficient facilities, and sourcing materials locally. For example, a company might redesign its distribution network to reduce its reliance on air freight, which has a high environmental impact, in favor of more sustainable modes of transportation like rail or sea.

Methodologies for Designing Distribution Networks

Several methodologies can be employed to design an optimal distribution network, each with its advantages and limitations. These methodologies are often used in combination to achieve the best results.

1. **Optimization Models:** These models use mathematical algorithms to find the best configuration of facilities, inventory levels, and transportation routes based on specific objectives, such as minimizing costs or maximizing service levels. Linear programming, mixed-integer programming, and network flow models are common techniques in this category. For example, a company might use a mixed-integer programming model to determine the ideal number and location of distribution centers that minimize total logistics costs while meeting service requirements.

2. **Simulation:** Simulation involves creating a digital model of the distribution network and testing various scenarios to evaluate their impact on performance. This approach allows companies to explore the effects of changes in demand, transportation disruptions, or facility closures without risking real-world consequences. For instance, a company might simulate the impact of a natural disaster on its distribution network to identify vulnerabilities and develop mitigation strategies.

3. **Heuristic Methods:** Heuristics are rules of thumb or simplified algorithms used to generate good, but not necessarily optimal, solutions quickly. These methods are particularly useful when dealing with large, complex networks where exact optimization would be computationally infeasible. A common heuristic in distribution network design is the "nearest neighbor" approach, which connects facilities in a way that minimizes the distance between them.

4. **Analytical Hierarchy Process (AHP):** AHP is a decision-making tool that helps prioritize multiple criteria by assigning weights to them. This method is useful when a company needs to balance several factors, such as cost, service level, and sustainability, in its network design. For example, a company might use AHP to rank potential distribution center locations based on factors like proximity to customers, labor availability, and environmental impact.

Real-World Examples of Successful Distribution Network Design

Several companies have successfully implemented innovative distribution network designs to achieve competitive advantages. One notable example is Zara, the global fashion retailer. Zara's distribution network is designed to support its fast fashion business model, which requires rapid turnover of inventory and quick response to changing fashion trends. Zara's distribution centers are centrally located in Spain, allowing the company to quickly distribute new products to its stores across Europe. This centralized approach enables Zara to maintain tight control over its inventory and respond rapidly to shifts in consumer demand.

Another example is Unilever, which has restructured its distribution network to enhance sustainability while maintaining cost efficiency. Unilever has implemented a "supply chain of the future" initiative, which involves consolidating its distribution centers into fewer, larger, and more automated facilities. This network design has reduced Unilever's carbon footprint by optimizing transportation routes and increasing the use of rail transport. At the same time, the company has improved service levels by reducing lead times and increasing product availability.

CHAPTER 3   LOGISTICS AND DISTRIBUTION MANAGEMENT

The Impact of Emerging Technologies on Distribution Network Design

The rise of digital technologies is transforming distribution network design, enabling more dynamic and responsive networks. Some of the key technologies driving this transformation include

1. **Artificial Intelligence (AI):** AI is being used to analyze vast amounts of data and generate insights that inform network design decisions. Machine learning algorithms can predict demand patterns, identify optimal facility locations, and recommend changes to the network in real time based on market conditions.

2. **Internet of Things (IoT):** IoT devices provide real-time visibility into the movement of goods, enabling companies to monitor their distribution networks more closely. For example, IoT sensors can track the location and condition of shipments, allowing companies to respond quickly to delays or disruptions.

3. **Blockchain:** Blockchain technology offers a secure, transparent way to track the movement of goods through the distribution network. This can enhance trust between supply chain partners and reduce the risk of fraud. Companies are beginning to experiment with blockchain to improve traceability and accountability in their networks.

4. **3D Printing:** While still in its early stages, 3D printing has the potential to disrupt distribution networks by enabling on-demand production closer to the point of consumption. This could reduce the need for large inventories and long-distance transportation, leading to more localized and responsive distribution networks.

By carefully considering factors such as customer demand, cost, service levels, and sustainability, companies can create networks that are efficient, resilient, and adaptable to change. As emerging technologies continue to evolve, the possibilities for optimizing distribution networks will expand, offering new opportunities for companies to gain a competitive edge. Whether through the use of AI, IoT, blockchain, or other innovations, the future of distribution network design promises to be dynamic and transformative.

3.5 Third-Party Logistics (3PL) and Fourth-Party Logistics (4PL)

These two logistics models represent different levels of outsourcing, where companies rely on external partners to handle various aspects of their logistics operations. As businesses strive to enhance efficiency, reduce costs, and adapt to complex global supply chains, 3PL and 4PL providers have emerged as indispensable partners in achieving these goals. This part delves into the intricacies of 3PL and 4PL, exploring their distinct roles, benefits, and the strategic impact they have on modern supply chains.

Understanding Third-Party Logistics (3PL)

Third-party logistics (3PL) refers to the outsourcing of specific logistics activities to external service providers. These activities typically include transportation, warehousing, inventory management, packaging, and sometimes even customs brokerage. The 3PL provider acts as an intermediary between the company and its customers, taking responsibility for the physical movement and storage of goods.

For example, a retail company might partner with a 3PL provider to manage its warehousing and distribution needs. Instead of investing in its own warehousing infrastructure and transportation fleet, the retailer relies on the 3PL provider's network of facilities and expertise to ensure that products are stored efficiently and delivered to customers on time. This allows the retailer to focus on its core competencies, such as marketing and product development, while the 3PL provider handles the logistics operations.

One of the primary advantages of 3PL is the ability to scale logistics operations according to demand. During peak seasons, such as the holiday shopping period, a company can leverage the 3PL provider's resources to handle increased order volumes without the need for significant capital investment. Conversely, during slower periods, the company can reduce its reliance on these services, thereby optimizing costs.

3PL providers also bring industry expertise and advanced technology to the table. They often use sophisticated logistics management systems (LMS) to optimize transportation routes, manage inventory levels, and track shipments in real time. By leveraging these tools, companies can improve supply chain visibility, enhance delivery accuracy, and reduce lead times.

However, while 3PL offers many benefits, it also presents challenges. Outsourcing logistics functions can lead to a loss of control over the supply chain, making it difficult for companies to ensure consistent service quality. Additionally, the reliance on a 3PL provider can create dependency, which may limit a company's flexibility to adapt to changing market conditions or customer demands.

The Evolution of Fourth-Party Logistics (4PL)

Fourth-party logistics (4PL) takes the concept of logistics outsourcing a step further. Unlike 3PL, where the focus is on the execution of logistics tasks, 4PL providers act as strategic partners that oversee and manage the entire supply chain on behalf of the company. This includes coordinating multiple 3PL providers, developing logistics strategies, and implementing end-to-end solutions that align with the company's business goals.

CHAPTER 3 LOGISTICS AND DISTRIBUTION MANAGEMENT

A 4PL provider essentially serves as a supply chain integrator, taking on a more consultative role. It works closely with the company to design and optimize the supply chain, identify opportunities for improvement, and ensure that all logistics activities are aligned with the overall business strategy. This can include everything from selecting the best 3PL partners to managing technology platforms and monitoring key performance indicators (KPIs).

For instance, a global electronics manufacturer might engage a 4PL provider to manage its entire supply chain, from sourcing raw materials to delivering finished products to retailers worldwide. The 4PL provider would be responsible for coordinating the efforts of multiple 3PL providers, optimizing transportation routes, managing inventory levels across different regions, and ensuring compliance with international trade regulations. By entrusting these complex logistics functions to a 4PL provider, the manufacturer can focus on innovation and product development, while benefiting from a streamlined and efficient supply chain.

The key advantage of 4PL is its ability to provide a holistic, end-to-end solution that enhances supply chain performance. By taking a strategic approach to logistics management, 4PL providers can identify inefficiencies, implement best practices, and drive continuous improvement across the supply chain. This can lead to significant cost savings, improved service levels, and greater agility in responding to market changes.

Moreover, 4PL providers often leverage advanced technologies, such as artificial intelligence (AI) and big data analytics, to gain deeper insights into supply chain operations. These technologies enable predictive analytics, which can anticipate demand fluctuations, identify potential disruptions, and recommend proactive measures to mitigate risks. As a result, companies can achieve greater supply chain resilience and responsiveness in an increasingly volatile global market.

Examples of 3PL and 4PL Success

The success of 3PL and 4PL models can be seen in numerous real-world examples. One such example is the partnership between Procter & Gamble (P&G) and DHL, a leading 3PL provider. P&G, one of the world's largest consumer goods companies, relies on DHL to manage its global distribution network. DHL handles everything from warehousing and transportation to order fulfillment and customs clearance. This partnership has enabled P&G to optimize its supply chain operations, reduce costs, and improve service levels, allowing the company to maintain its competitive edge in the global market.

In the realm of 4PL, the partnership between Unilever and Accenture stands out. Unilever, a global leader in consumer goods, engaged Accenture as its 4PL provider to transform its supply chain operations. Accenture took on the role of supply chain integrator, overseeing the entire logistics network, coordinating multiple 3PL providers, and implementing advanced analytics to drive performance improvements. As a result, Unilever achieved greater supply chain visibility, reduced lead times, and enhanced its ability to respond to changing market demands.

These examples highlight the transformative impact that 3PL and 4PL providers can have on supply chain performance. By leveraging the expertise, resources, and technology of these external partners, companies can achieve greater efficiency, flexibility, and scalability in their logistics operations.

The Future of 3PL and 4PL

As supply chains continue to evolve in response to globalization, e-commerce growth, and technological advancements, the roles of 3PL and 4PL providers are likely to become even more critical. Companies will increasingly rely on these partners to navigate the complexities of global logistics, manage risk, and drive innovation.

In the future, we can expect to see 3PL and 4PL providers expanding their service offerings to include more value-added services, such as reverse logistics, sustainability initiatives, and digital supply chain solutions. The integration of emerging technologies, such as blockchain, IoT, and AI, will further enhance the capabilities of these providers, enabling them to offer more sophisticated and data-driven solutions.

Furthermore, the distinction between 3PL and 4PL may become less clear as providers increasingly offer hybrid models that combine the operational focus of 3PL with the strategic oversight of 4PL. This evolution will create new opportunities for companies to optimize their supply chains and achieve greater competitive advantage.

Third-party logistics (3PL) and fourth-party logistics (4PL) are powerful tools for companies seeking to optimize their supply chain operations. While 3PL providers focus on executing specific logistics tasks, 4PL providers take a more strategic approach, managing the entire supply chain on behalf of the company. Both models offer significant benefits, including cost savings, enhanced efficiency, and greater supply chain resilience. As supply chains become more complex and dynamic, the role of 3PL and 4PL providers will continue to evolve, offering new opportunities for companies to achieve operational excellence and drive business growth.

3.6 Reverse Logistics

Reverse logistics refers to the process of moving goods from their final destination back to the manufacturer or a designated facility for returns, repairs, refurbishment, recycling, or disposal. This chapter delves into the complexities of reverse logistics, exploring its significance, challenges, and the innovative strategies companies are using to transform returns into revenue opportunities.

The Growing Importance of Reverse Logistics

Traditionally, logistics has focused on the forward movement of products—from the production line to the consumer's hands. However, as consumer expectations evolve and the demand for sustainability grows, reverse logistics has gained prominence. The rise of e-commerce has also played a significant role in this shift. Online shopping has made it easier for consumers to return products, resulting in an increase in the volume of returns that companies must handle. In some sectors, return rates can exceed 30%, making reverse logistics a critical area of focus.

Reverse logistics is not just about managing returns; it's about optimizing the process to reduce costs, minimize waste, and recover value. Effective reverse logistics can enhance customer satisfaction by ensuring that returns are processed quickly and efficiently, leading to positive customer experiences and increased loyalty. Additionally, it can contribute to sustainability efforts by facilitating the reuse, recycling, and proper disposal of products, thus reducing the environmental impact.

Key Components of Reverse Logistics

Reverse logistics encompasses a wide range of activities, each with its own set of challenges and opportunities. These include

1. **Returns Management**: This is the core of reverse logistics. It involves handling the return of products from customers, whether due to defects, damage, dissatisfaction, or simply a change of mind. Efficient returns management requires a well-coordinated system that can process returns quickly, provide refunds or replacements, and manage inventory effectively.

Example: A fashion retailer might implement a streamlined returns process that allows customers to easily return items by mail or in-store. The retailer uses an automated system to track returns, update inventory, and issue refunds, ensuring a seamless experience for the customer.

2. **Remanufacturing and Refurbishment**: Products that are returned in good condition or with minor defects can be remanufactured or refurbished for resale. This process involves inspecting, repairing, and restoring the product to like-new condition. Remanufacturing not only reduces waste but also provides an opportunity to generate additional revenue from returned products.

   Example: A leading electronics company receives a high volume of returns for its smartphones. Rather than discarding these devices, the company refurbishes them and sells them at a discounted price through its online store, appealing to cost-conscious consumers while maximizing revenue.

3. **Recycling and Disposal**: Products that cannot be resold or refurbished must be recycled or disposed of in an environmentally responsible manner. Recycling involves breaking down the product into its component materials, which can then be used to create new products. Proper disposal ensures that hazardous materials are handled safely and do not harm the environment.

   Example: A manufacturer of home appliances partners with a recycling firm to ensure that returned products that are no longer functional are dismantled and recycled. The metals, plastics, and other materials are separated and reintroduced into the manufacturing process, reducing the need for virgin materials.

4. **Asset Recovery**: This refers to the process of recovering value from returned, excess, or obsolete products. This can be done through resale, recycling, or even repurposing products for other uses. Asset recovery helps companies minimize losses and maximize the return on their investments in inventory.

   Example: A tech company regularly updates its inventory of servers and networking equipment. Rather than discarding outdated equipment, the company sells it to a third-party reseller, recovering a portion of its investment while freeing up space for new inventory.

5. **Waste Management**: In reverse logistics, waste management is crucial for ensuring that products and materials that cannot be reused or recycled are disposed of in a way that minimizes environmental impact. Companies must comply with regulations and standards related to the disposal of electronic waste, hazardous materials, and other potentially harmful substances.

   Example: A chemical manufacturer implements a comprehensive waste management program that includes the safe disposal of expired or unused chemicals. The company works with certified disposal firms to ensure that hazardous materials are handled in compliance with environmental regulations.

Challenges in Reverse Logistics

While reverse logistics offers numerous benefits, it also presents several challenges. One of the primary challenges is the complexity of managing returns, which can vary significantly depending on the product, customer, and reason for return. Unlike forward logistics, which typically follows a predictable path, reverse logistics is often unpredictable, with variations in the condition of returned products, fluctuating volumes, and varying customer expectations.

Another challenge is the cost associated with reverse logistics. Processing returns, refurbishing products, and managing waste all incur costs, and companies must find ways to optimize these processes to minimize expenses while maintaining quality and customer satisfaction. Additionally, the integration of reverse logistics with existing supply chain systems can be complex, requiring investment in technology and training.

Furthermore, reverse logistics requires effective coordination with multiple stakeholders, including customers, suppliers, logistics providers, and recycling firms. This coordination is essential for ensuring that returns are processed efficiently, products are refurbished or recycled properly, and waste is managed in an environmentally responsible manner.

Innovative Strategies in Reverse Logistics

Despite the challenges, companies are finding innovative ways to turn reverse logistics into a competitive advantage. One such strategy is the use of advanced analytics to optimize returns management. By analyzing data on returns, companies can identify patterns and trends that help them reduce return rates, improve product quality, and enhance customer satisfaction.

Another strategy is the adoption of circular economy principles, where products are designed with their entire life cycle in mind. This includes designing products that are easier to repair, refurbish, and recycle, thus extending their useful life and reducing waste. Companies are also exploring new business models, such as product-as-a-service, where customers pay for the use of a product rather than owning it outright. This model encourages the return of products at the end of their useful life, facilitating refurbishment and reuse.

The Future of Reverse Logistics

As sustainability becomes increasingly important to consumers and regulators, reverse logistics will continue to evolve and expand in scope. Companies that excel in reverse logistics will not only reduce costs and recover value but also enhance their reputation as responsible and sustainable businesses. The integration of technology, such as IoT and blockchain, will further enhance the efficiency and transparency of reverse logistics processes, enabling companies to track products throughout their life cycle and ensure they are handled in accordance with environmental and regulatory standards.

Reverse logistics is more than just a cost center; it is a critical component of modern supply chain management that can drive profitability, customer satisfaction, and sustainability. By embracing the challenges and opportunities of reverse logistics, companies can turn returns into revenue and build a more resilient and responsible supply chain.

CHAPTER 4

Supply Chain Integration and Collaboration

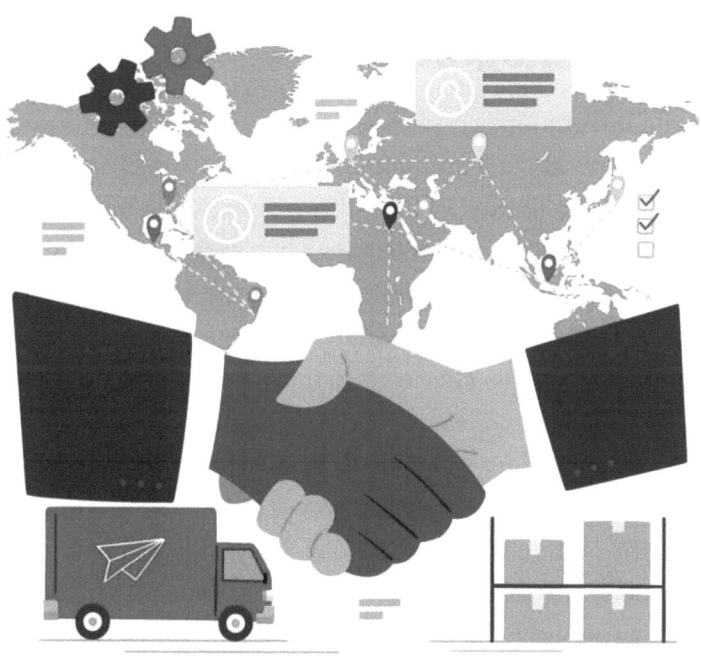

Figure 4-1. Supply Chain Integration and Collaboration

CHAPTER 4   SUPPLY CHAIN INTEGRATION AND COLLABORATION

As companies strive to deliver products faster, cheaper, and with greater precision, the need for effective supply chain integration and collaboration has never been more critical. Supply chain integration refers to the alignment and seamless coordination of all the activities, processes, and stakeholders involved in the supply chain, from raw material suppliers to end customers. Meanwhile, collaboration involves the cooperation between different entities in the supply chain, including suppliers, manufacturers, distributors, retailers, and even competitors, to achieve common goals. This chapter explores the significance of supply chain integration and collaboration, the strategies to achieve it, and the benefits it brings to organizations.

4.1 The Importance of Supply Chain Integration

Supply chain integration is essential for creating a cohesive and efficient supply chain network. In a traditional supply chain, each entity operates independently, with limited visibility into the activities and needs of others. This often leads to inefficiencies, such as delays, stockouts, excess inventory, and increased costs. By integrating the supply chain, companies can synchronize their operations, share real-time information, and make more informed decisions. This leads to improved efficiency, reduced costs, and enhanced responsiveness to market changes.

For example, consider a global electronics manufacturer that sources components from multiple suppliers across different countries. Without integration, the manufacturer might face delays due to a lack of visibility into the supplier's production schedules or shipping timelines. By integrating its supply chain, the manufacturer can access real-time data on supplier inventory levels, production status, and shipping updates, allowing it to adjust its production plans and avoid costly delays.

4.2 Strategies for Achieving Supply Chain Integration

Achieving supply chain integration requires a combination of technological, organizational, and strategic initiatives. Here are some key strategies:

1. **Adoption of Technology**: Technology plays a crucial role in supply chain integration. Enterprise Resource Planning (ERP) systems, Supply Chain Management (SCM) software, and other digital tools enable companies to centralize data, automate processes, and enhance visibility across the supply chain. For instance, an ERP system can integrate all the core functions of a company—such as procurement, production, sales, and logistics—into a single platform, ensuring that all departments are aligned and working toward the same goals.

2. **Data Sharing and Communication**: Effective communication and data sharing are the cornerstones of supply chain integration. Companies need to establish robust communication channels with their suppliers, customers, and other stakeholders. This includes sharing forecasts, inventory levels, production plans, and delivery schedules. Real-time data sharing enables companies to anticipate demand, manage inventory efficiently, and respond quickly to disruptions. For example, a retailer might share its sales data with suppliers, allowing them to adjust their production schedules and reduce lead times.

3. **Process Standardization**: Standardizing processes across the supply chain is another key strategy for integration. When all entities in the supply chain follow the same processes and standards, it becomes easier to coordinate activities, reduce errors, and improve efficiency. This can involve standardizing order processing, inventory management, quality control, and transportation procedures. For example, a global automotive manufacturer might standardize its quality control processes across all its suppliers to ensure consistency in the quality of components used in its vehicles.

4. **Cross-Functional Teams**: Creating cross-functional teams that include representatives from different departments—such as procurement, production, logistics, and sales—can facilitate better coordination and decision-making. These teams can work together to address supply chain challenges, such as demand fluctuations, production bottlenecks, and supplier issues. For instance, a consumer goods company might form a cross-functional team to manage the launch of a new product, ensuring that all aspects of the supply chain are aligned to meet the launch date.

5. **Long-Term Partnerships with Suppliers**: Building long-term relationships with key suppliers is essential for supply chain integration. When companies work closely with their suppliers, they can develop trust, improve communication, and align their goals. This can lead to better

collaboration on product development, cost reduction, and process improvement. For example, a pharmaceutical company might collaborate with its key suppliers to develop new packaging materials that reduce costs and improve sustainability.

4.3 The Role of Collaboration in Supply Chain Integration

Collaboration is the driving force behind successful supply chain integration. In today's competitive business environment, companies can no longer afford to operate in silos. Collaboration involves working together with supply chain partners to achieve common objectives, such as reducing costs, improving quality, and enhancing customer satisfaction. This requires a shift in mindset from viewing suppliers and competitors as adversaries to seeing them as partners in achieving mutual success.

4.4 Benefits of Supply Chain Integration and Collaboration

The benefits of supply chain integration and collaboration are numerous and far-reaching. Here are some of the key advantages:

1. **Improved Efficiency**: Integrated supply chains are more efficient because they eliminate redundancies, reduce lead times, and streamline processes. This leads to cost savings and better utilization of resources. For example, by integrating its supply chain, a manufacturer can reduce the time it takes to move materials from suppliers to production lines, leading to faster production cycles.

2. **Enhanced Responsiveness**: An integrated supply chain is more responsive to changes in demand, market conditions, and customer preferences. This agility allows companies to quickly adjust their production plans, inventory levels, and distribution strategies, ensuring that they can meet customer needs without incurring excessive costs. For instance, a fashion retailer might use real-time sales data to adjust its inventory levels in response to changing trends, ensuring that popular items are always in stock.

3. **Increased Customer Satisfaction**: When companies collaborate effectively and integrate their supply chains, they can deliver products to customers faster, with fewer errors, and at a lower cost. This leads to higher levels of customer satisfaction and loyalty. For example, an e-commerce company might work closely with its logistics partners to ensure that orders are delivered quickly and accurately, leading to positive customer reviews and repeat business.

4. **Risk Mitigation**: Supply chain integration and collaboration can help companies identify and mitigate risks more effectively. By sharing information and working together, companies can anticipate potential disruptions, such as supplier shortages, transportation delays, or geopolitical events, and take proactive measures to address them. For instance, a global electronics

manufacturer might collaborate with its suppliers to develop contingency plans in case of a natural disaster that disrupts production in a key region.

5. **Innovation and Continuous Improvement**: Collaboration fosters innovation by bringing together different perspectives, expertise, and resources. When companies work together, they can develop new products, processes, and technologies that improve the overall performance of the supply chain. For example, a food and beverage company might collaborate with its packaging suppliers to develop eco-friendly packaging that reduces waste and meets consumer demand for sustainable products.

4.5 The Importance of Integration in Supply Chains

Companies are no longer confined to local markets; they are sourcing, manufacturing, and distributing products across multiple continents. With such a vast network of suppliers, manufacturers, logistics providers, and retailers, the challenge of maintaining an efficient, responsive, and cost-effective supply chain is greater than ever. Integration in supply chains has emerged as a critical solution to this challenge. Supply chain integration involves the coordination and alignment of processes, technologies, and stakeholders across the entire supply chain, from raw material suppliers to end customers. This chapter delves into the importance of integration in supply chains, examining how it drives efficiency, reduces costs, enhances agility, and fosters innovation.

CHAPTER 4   SUPPLY CHAIN INTEGRATION AND COLLABORATION

Driving Efficiency Through Integration

One of the most significant benefits of supply chain integration is the dramatic improvement in efficiency. In traditional supply chains, each entity operates in a silo, often leading to duplicated efforts, communication breakdowns, and misaligned objectives. This lack of coordination results in inefficiencies such as excess inventory, delayed deliveries, and higher operational costs.

Integration breaks down these silos by fostering collaboration and communication across the supply chain. For instance, consider a multinational consumer electronics company that sources components from multiple suppliers around the world. Without integration, each supplier might work independently, leading to mismatched production schedules and delayed shipments. However, by integrating its supply chain, the company can synchronize its production schedules with its suppliers, ensuring that components are delivered just in time for assembly, thereby reducing inventory costs and speeding up time-to-market.

A real-life example of this is Dell's build-to-order model, which relies heavily on supply chain integration. Dell's suppliers are closely integrated into its supply chain, providing real-time updates on inventory levels and production capabilities. This integration allows Dell to assemble computers based on customer orders rather than forecasts, reducing inventory costs and enabling rapid response to customer demand.

Reducing Costs and Enhancing Profitability

Cost reduction is a primary driver for companies seeking to integrate their supply chains. By streamlining operations and eliminating redundancies, integration helps companies reduce both direct and indirect costs. For example, when suppliers, manufacturers, and logistics providers are integrated into a single, cohesive network, companies can optimize transportation routes, consolidate shipments, and negotiate better rates with carriers, leading to significant savings.

Furthermore, integration enables better demand forecasting and inventory management, which are critical for reducing holding costs and minimizing stockouts. For example, a retailer with an integrated supply chain can share sales data with suppliers in real time, allowing them to adjust their production schedules and inventory levels accordingly. This not only reduces the cost of holding excess inventory but also minimizes the risk of lost sales due to stockouts.

A case in point is the collaboration between Walmart and its suppliers. Walmart's Retail Link system, an integrated supply chain platform, allows suppliers to access real-time sales data and manage their inventory levels accordingly. This integration has helped Walmart achieve one of the lowest cost structures in the retail industry, allowing it to offer competitive prices to customers while maintaining healthy profit margins.

Enhancing Agility and Responsiveness

Agility and responsiveness are crucial for staying competitive. Companies must be able to quickly adapt to fluctuations in demand, changes in consumer preferences, and disruptions in the supply chain. Supply chain integration enhances agility by enabling real-time information sharing, collaborative planning, and flexible production processes.

For example, during the COVID-19 pandemic, many companies faced significant disruptions in their supply chains. Those with integrated supply chains were better equipped to respond to these challenges. By sharing information across the supply chain, companies were able to identify potential bottlenecks, reroute shipments, and adjust production schedules in real time. This level of agility allowed them to continue serving customers despite the disruptions.

An example of this is the automotive industry, which faced severe disruptions due to the pandemic. Companies like Toyota, which had invested in supply chain integration, were able to quickly identify alternative suppliers and adjust production schedules to meet changing demands. This agility allowed Toyota to minimize the impact of the disruptions and continue delivering vehicles to customers.

Fostering Innovation and Competitive Advantage

Integration in supply chains is not just about efficiency and cost reduction; it also plays a crucial role in fostering innovation and gaining a competitive advantage. When companies integrate their supply chains, they create an environment where collaboration and knowledge sharing can thrive. This collaborative approach often leads to the development of new products, processes, and technologies that can differentiate a company from its competitors.

For instance, consider the collaboration between Apple and its suppliers. Apple's integrated supply chain allows it to work closely with suppliers to develop innovative components for its products. This close collaboration has resulted in the development of cutting-edge technologies, such as the Retina display and the A-series processors, which have helped Apple maintain its position as a leader in the consumer electronics market.

The Future of Supply Chain Integration

As supply chains become more complex and global, the importance of integration will continue to grow. Advances in digital technologies, such as artificial intelligence (AI), blockchain, and the Internet of Things (IoT), are poised to further enhance supply chain integration by providing unprecedented levels of visibility, automation, and predictive capabilities.

For example, AI can analyze vast amounts of data from across the supply chain to identify patterns, predict demand, and optimize operations. Blockchain technology can enhance transparency and trust by providing a secure, immutable record of transactions across the supply chain. Meanwhile, IoT devices can provide real-time data on the location and condition of goods as they move through the supply chain, enabling companies to monitor and manage their supply chains more effectively.

Supply chain integration is a critical driver of efficiency, cost reduction, agility, innovation, and competitive advantage. As companies continue to navigate the challenges of a globalized economy, those that invest in integrating their supply chains will be better positioned to succeed in the long term. By embracing integration, companies can create a seamless, responsive, and resilient supply chain that meets the demands of today's dynamic market environment.

4.6 Collaborative Planning, Forecasting, and Replenishment (CPFR)

Collaborative Planning, Forecasting, and Replenishment (CPFR) has emerged as a strategic approach to drive superior performance. CPFR is a business practice that combines the intelligence of multiple trading partners in the planning and fulfillment of customer demand. This approach goes beyond the traditional boundaries of supply chain management, fostering a closer relationship between manufacturers, suppliers, and retailers. It's a holistic, integrated process that seeks to improve supply chain accuracy, efficiency, and customer satisfaction.

CHAPTER 4   SUPPLY CHAIN INTEGRATION AND COLLABORATION

The Essence of CPFR

At its core, CPFR is about collaboration—bringing together all key stakeholders in the supply chain to share information, align objectives, and coordinate activities. The traditional approach to supply chain management often involves each entity operating in silos, leading to inefficiencies, misaligned goals, and suboptimal decision-making. CPFR, on the other hand, promotes transparency and communication, ensuring that all parties are on the same page regarding demand forecasts, production plans, inventory levels, and replenishment schedules.

The process typically involves several key steps: collaboration agreement, joint business planning, demand forecasting, order planning, and execution, as well as performance assessment. By engaging in these activities collectively, supply chain partners can synchronize their operations, reduce uncertainties, and respond more effectively to changes in market demand.

Improving Demand Forecasting Accuracy

One of the most significant benefits of CPFR is the improvement in demand forecasting accuracy. Accurate demand forecasting is crucial for ensuring that the right products are available at the right time and place, minimizing stockouts and excess inventory. However, traditional forecasting methods often fall short due to a lack of visibility across the supply chain and insufficient communication between partners.

CPFR addresses this challenge by enabling trading partners to share their insights and data. For example, a retailer might have access to real-time sales data and customer trends, while a manufacturer might possess historical production data and market intelligence. By combining these perspectives, CPFR allows for more accurate and reliable demand forecasts.

Consider the example of Walmart, which has been a pioneer in adopting CPFR practices. By collaborating closely with suppliers like Procter & Gamble (P&G), Walmart has been able to significantly improve its demand forecasting accuracy. P&G shares its sales data and promotional plans with Walmart, allowing both companies to align their production schedules and inventory management. This collaboration has led to reduced stockouts, optimized inventory levels, and increased sales for both parties.

Enhancing Supply Chain Agility

In today's fast-paced market environment, supply chain agility—the ability to quickly adapt to changes in demand, supply disruptions, and other external factors—is critical for maintaining a competitive edge. CPFR enhances supply chain agility by fostering real-time communication and collaboration among trading partners.

For instance, when a retailer notices a sudden spike in demand for a particular product, it can immediately share this information with the manufacturer through the CPFR process. The manufacturer, in turn, can adjust its production schedule and order more raw materials to meet the increased demand. Similarly, if a supplier faces a disruption, such as a shortage of raw materials or a logistical delay, it can inform its partners through the CPFR platform, allowing them to take proactive measures to mitigate the impact.

An illustrative example of CPFR in action is the partnership between Kimberly-Clark and its retail partners. By using CPFR to share real-time data and collaborate on demand forecasts, Kimberly-Clark has been able to respond quickly to changes in demand, reducing lead times and improving product availability on store shelves. This agility has not only enhanced customer satisfaction but also driven growth in sales and market share.

Optimizing Inventory Management

Effective inventory management is a critical aspect of supply chain performance, impacting both costs and service levels. Poor inventory management can lead to excess stock, which ties up capital and increases storage costs, or stockouts, which result in lost sales and dissatisfied customers. CPFR offers a solution to these challenges by enabling more precise inventory planning and replenishment.

Through CPFR, trading partners can collaborate on inventory policies, such as reorder points, safety stock levels, and order quantities. This collaboration ensures that inventory levels are optimized across the supply chain, reducing the risk of stockouts and overstock situations. Additionally, CPFR allows for continuous monitoring and adjustment of inventory plans based on real-time demand data and market conditions.

For example, the collaboration between Coca-Cola and its bottling partners demonstrates the effectiveness of CPFR in optimizing inventory management. By sharing demand forecasts and inventory data, Coca-Cola and its bottlers have been able to synchronize production and distribution, ensuring that the right amount of product is available at the right time. This collaboration has led to lower inventory costs, reduced waste, and improved service levels, contributing to Coca-Cola's success in the highly competitive beverage market.

Strengthening Relationships and Trust

CPFR not only drives operational efficiencies but also strengthens relationships and trust between trading partners. In a traditional supply chain, relationships are often transactional, with each party focused on maximizing its own interests. CPFR, however, encourages a more collaborative and transparent approach, where partners work together to achieve shared goals.

By engaging in CPFR, companies can build stronger, more strategic relationships with their suppliers, manufacturers, and retailers. This collaboration fosters a sense of mutual trust and commitment, leading to more effective problem-solving, innovation, and long-term partnerships.

A case in point is the collaboration between Nestlé and its key suppliers. Through CPFR, Nestlé has been able to build strong, trust-based relationships with its suppliers, enabling greater collaboration on product development, supply chain innovation, and sustainability initiatives. This collaborative approach has not only improved supply chain performance but also strengthened Nestlé's reputation as a reliable and responsible business partner.

The Future of CPFR

For instance, AI can analyze vast amounts of data from across the supply chain to identify patterns, predict demand, and optimize replenishment strategies. Machine learning algorithms can continuously improve forecasting accuracy by learning from past data and adjusting models in real time. Blockchain technology can enhance trust and transparency in the CPFR process by providing a secure, immutable record of transactions and data exchanges.

CPFR is a powerful approach to supply chain management that offers significant benefits in terms of demand forecasting accuracy, supply chain agility, inventory management, and relationship building. By embracing CPFR, companies can create more responsive, efficient, and collaborative supply chains that are better equipped to meet the demands of today's dynamic market environment. As digital technologies continue to advance, the potential for CPFR to drive even greater value in supply chain management will only grow, making it a critical strategy for businesses seeking to thrive in the future.

4.7 Supplier Relationship Management (SRM)

The goal of SRM is to streamline and make these processes more effective, fostering closer, more collaborative relationships between an organization and its suppliers. Unlike traditional procurement, which often focuses on cost reduction and transactional efficiency, SRM emphasizes long-term value creation and mutual benefits. By building stronger relationships with suppliers, companies can gain competitive advantages, such as increased innovation, better quality, and improved sustainability.

The Strategic Importance of SRM

In today's globalized and complex supply chains, the role of suppliers has evolved from mere vendors to strategic partners. Companies increasingly rely on their suppliers not just for raw materials or services but also for innovation, flexibility, and risk management. This shift has made SRM a critical component of supply chain management.

One of the primary reasons SRM is so important is its impact on risk management. In a world where supply chain disruptions can occur due to geopolitical tensions, natural disasters, or economic shifts, having strong relationships with key suppliers can help companies navigate these challenges more effectively. For instance, during the COVID-19 pandemic, companies that had established strong SRM practices were better able to secure necessary supplies and maintain operations compared to those that treated their suppliers purely as transactional entities.

A real-world example of effective SRM can be seen in Toyota's relationship with its suppliers. Toyota's SRM approach is based on the concept of "kyoryoku kai," or supplier associations, where the company and its suppliers work closely together to improve product quality, reduce costs, and innovate. This collaborative approach has been a key factor in Toyota's ability to consistently deliver high-quality vehicles while maintaining a competitive edge in the automotive industry.

Building Strong Supplier Relationships

Building strong supplier relationships requires more than just signing contracts and negotiating prices. It involves a commitment to collaboration, communication, and mutual growth. The foundation of SRM is trust, and trust is built through transparency, reliability, and a shared vision for success.

One of the first steps in building strong supplier relationships is to segment suppliers based on their strategic importance. Not all suppliers require the same level of attention, and companies need to identify which suppliers are critical to their operations and which can be managed with a more transactional approach. For example, a supplier that provides a unique, high-value component may be considered a strategic partner, while a supplier of generic office supplies may not.

Once key suppliers are identified, the next step is to establish clear expectations and goals. This involves setting up regular communication channels, defining performance metrics, and working together to align objectives. A good example of this is Apple's relationship with its suppliers, particularly those involved in the production of the iPhone. Apple works closely with its suppliers, providing them with detailed specifications, ongoing support, and even investing in their capabilities to ensure that they can meet Apple's stringent quality and innovation standards.

Driving Innovation through SRM

One of the most significant benefits of SRM is its potential to drive innovation. By fostering closer relationships with suppliers, companies can tap into their suppliers' expertise, resources, and ideas, leading to the development of new products, processes, or services. This collaborative innovation is particularly important in industries where technology and customer preferences are rapidly evolving.

For example, Procter & Gamble (P&G) has long recognized the value of supplier-driven innovation. The company actively involves its suppliers in the product development process, encouraging them to bring new ideas and technologies to the table. This approach has led to several successful product innovations, such as the development of the Swiffer cleaning products, which was a result of close collaboration between P&G and one of its key suppliers.

Innovation through SRM isn't limited to product development. It can also extend to process improvements, such as more efficient manufacturing techniques or more sustainable sourcing practices. For instance, Unilever's partnership with its palm oil suppliers has led to significant advancements in sustainable sourcing. By working closely with these suppliers, Unilever has been able to develop and implement more sustainable practices, reducing deforestation and improving the livelihoods of smallholder farmers.

Enhancing Supplier Performance and Accountability

Another critical aspect of SRM is enhancing supplier performance and accountability. To ensure that suppliers meet the organization's standards and expectations, companies must establish clear performance metrics and regularly monitor supplier performance. This includes metrics related to quality, delivery, cost, and compliance with sustainability and ethical standards.

One effective tool for managing supplier performance is the use of scorecards. Supplier scorecards provide a standardized way to evaluate and compare suppliers based on key performance indicators (KPIs). These scorecards can be shared with suppliers to provide them with feedback and help them understand where they need to improve. For example, Coca-Cola uses supplier scorecards to assess the performance of its bottling partners. By providing regular feedback and setting clear expectations, Coca-Cola has been able to maintain high standards of quality and efficiency across its global supply chain.

In addition to performance monitoring, SRM also involves holding suppliers accountable for their actions. This means that companies must be willing to address issues such as quality failures, delivery delays, or noncompliance with ethical standards. However, accountability in SRM is not about punishment; it's about working with suppliers to identify root causes of problems and collaboratively finding solutions. For example, if a supplier consistently fails to meet delivery deadlines, the company might work with the supplier to identify bottlenecks in their production process and provide support to help them improve.

The Future of SRM: Digital Transformation

As with many aspects of supply chain management, SRM is being transformed by digital technologies. Digital tools and platforms are making it easier for companies to manage their supplier relationships, from onboarding and performance tracking to collaboration and innovation.

One of the most significant advancements in SRM is the use of blockchain technology. Blockchain provides a secure, transparent, and immutable record of transactions and interactions between companies and their suppliers. This technology can enhance trust and accountability in SRM by providing real-time visibility into the supply chain and ensuring that all parties have access to the same accurate information. For example, IBM has developed a blockchain-based platform called IBM Food Trust, which allows companies to trace the origins of food products through the supply chain, enhancing transparency and trust between suppliers and retailers.

Another emerging trend in SRM is the use of artificial intelligence (AI) and machine learning. These technologies can analyze vast amounts of data from suppliers to identify patterns, predict potential risks, and optimize supplier performance. For instance, AI can be used to analyze supplier performance data and predict which suppliers are most likely to experience disruptions, allowing companies to proactively address these risks.

Supplier relationship management is a critical aspect of modern supply chain management that goes beyond transactional interactions to build long-term, strategic partnerships. By focusing on collaboration, innovation, and performance, companies can create more resilient, efficient, and sustainable supply chains. As digital technologies continue to evolve, the potential for SRM to drive even greater value will only increase, making it a key area of focus for organizations seeking to maintain a competitive edge in the future.

4.8 Information Sharing and Coordination

Information sharing and coordination are not just operational necessities; they are strategic imperatives that can significantly enhance efficiency, reduce costs, and improve service levels. In a supply chain, information is the lifeblood that connects various entities—from suppliers and manufacturers to distributors and retailers—ensuring that every part of the system is informed and synchronized.

Information sharing involves the dissemination of relevant data, such as demand forecasts, inventory levels, production schedules, and delivery statuses, among all parties in the supply chain. Coordination, on the other hand, is the alignment of activities and processes based on this shared information. Together, they enable supply chain participants to operate more effectively, respond swiftly to changes, and make informed decisions that benefit the entire network.

The Strategic Importance of Information Sharing

The importance of information sharing in supply chains cannot be overstated. When information flows freely and accurately, it reduces uncertainty and allows for better planning and decision-making. Companies that excel in information sharing are often better equipped to forecast demand, optimize inventory levels, and reduce lead times, leading to a more efficient and responsive supply chain.

One of the most significant examples of effective information sharing is seen in the partnership between Walmart and Procter & Gamble (P&G). This collaboration is often cited as a benchmark for supply chain excellence. Walmart, one of the world's largest retailers, and P&G, a leading consumer goods manufacturer, have implemented a system where data on sales and inventory levels at Walmart stores is shared directly with P&G. This real-time data allows P&G to adjust its production and distribution plans to meet Walmart's needs more accurately, reducing stockouts and excess inventory. The result is a highly synchronized supply chain that benefits both companies through lower costs and improved customer satisfaction.

However, the benefits of information sharing extend beyond operational efficiency. It also fosters stronger relationships between supply chain partners. When companies share information transparently, they build trust and collaboration, which are essential for long-term partnerships. Trust encourages suppliers and manufacturers to work more closely, share risks, and innovate together, ultimately leading to a more resilient and competitive supply chain.

CHAPTER 4   SUPPLY CHAIN INTEGRATION AND COLLABORATION

Overcoming Barriers to Information Sharing

Despite its clear advantages, information sharing in supply chains is often hindered by several challenges. One of the most significant barriers is the lack of trust between supply chain partners. Companies may be reluctant to share sensitive data, fearing that it could be used against them or shared with competitors. This lack of trust can lead to a siloed approach where each entity in the supply chain operates in isolation, leading to inefficiencies and misaligned objectives.

To overcome this barrier, companies need to invest in building trust with their partners. This can be achieved through transparency, clear communication, and the establishment of mutually beneficial goals. For example, Toyota has successfully cultivated trust with its suppliers by involving them in the product development process and sharing long-term forecasts. This collaboration has led to the development of high-quality products and more efficient manufacturing processes, benefiting both Toyota and its suppliers.

Another challenge to information sharing is the lack of standardized data formats and systems across the supply chain. When different companies use incompatible systems or data formats, it becomes difficult to share information effectively. To address this issue, companies can adopt industry standards for data exchange or invest in integrated supply chain management systems that facilitate seamless communication. The automotive industry, for instance, has made significant strides in standardizing data formats through initiatives like the Automotive Industry Action Group (AIAG), which has developed common standards for data exchange among automakers and suppliers.

The Role of Technology in Enhancing Information Sharing

Advancements in technology have played a crucial role in enhancing information sharing and coordination in supply chains. Digital tools such as cloud computing, the Internet of Things (IoT), and blockchain are transforming how information is shared and used across supply chains.

Cloud-based platforms, for example, provide a centralized repository for data, accessible to all authorized parties in real time. These platforms enable companies to share information on demand, inventory levels, and production schedules more efficiently. For instance, Cisco Systems uses a cloud-based platform to manage its global supply chain. The platform allows Cisco to share real-time information with its suppliers and partners, leading to better demand forecasting, reduced lead times, and more agile decision-making.

IoT devices also play a critical role in improving information sharing. By collecting and transmitting data from various points in the supply chain, IoT devices provide real-time visibility into the status of shipments, inventory levels, and equipment performance. This real-time data enables companies to monitor their supply chains more closely, identify potential issues before they escalate, and make proactive adjustments. A notable example is Maersk, the global shipping giant, which uses IoT technology to monitor the location, temperature, and humidity of its containers. This information is shared with customers and partners, allowing them to track their shipments in real time and ensure the quality of perishable goods.

Blockchain technology is another innovation that enhances information sharing by providing a secure, transparent, and immutable record of transactions and data exchanges. Blockchain's decentralized nature ensures that all parties in the supply chain have access to the same information, reducing the risk of disputes and ensuring data integrity. For example, IBM and Walmart have collaborated to implement a blockchain-based system for tracking food products through the supply chain. This system allows Walmart to trace the origin of food items quickly in case of a recall, improving food safety and reducing waste.

The Impact of Information Sharing on Supply Chain Performance

Effective information sharing and coordination have a profound impact on overall supply chain performance. When companies share information openly and coordinate their activities, they can achieve greater alignment of supply and demand, reduce lead times, and improve customer service levels.

For example, Dell's direct-to-consumer business model relies heavily on information sharing and coordination with its suppliers. By sharing real-time sales data and forecasts with its suppliers, Dell can keep inventory levels low while ensuring that components are available when needed. This approach has allowed Dell to offer customized products with shorter lead times, giving it a competitive advantage in the technology market.

Moreover, information sharing can lead to cost savings by reducing the need for safety stock and minimizing the bullwhip effect, where small fluctuations in demand lead to larger variations in orders upstream in the supply chain. By providing accurate and timely information, companies can better match production with actual demand, reducing excess inventory and associated carrying costs.

In addition to operational benefits, information sharing can also lead to greater innovation and sustainability in supply chains. When companies collaborate closely and share information on new technologies, materials, and processes, they can develop more innovative products and solutions. For instance, Unilever has collaborated with its suppliers to develop sustainable packaging solutions, sharing information on material specifications, manufacturing processes, and supply chain impacts. This collaboration has led to the introduction of more environmentally friendly products, enhancing Unilever's brand reputation and meeting consumer demands for sustainability.

The Future of Information Sharing and Coordination

As supply chains become more complex and global, the importance of information sharing and coordination will continue to grow. Companies that invest in building trust with their partners, adopting standardized data formats, and leveraging digital technologies will be better positioned to compete in this dynamic environment.

The future of supply chain management lies in the ability to share information seamlessly across the entire network, enabling real-time visibility, agile decision-making, and collaborative innovation. By embracing these principles, companies can create more resilient, efficient, and sustainable supply chains that drive long-term success.

4.9 Risk Management in Supply Chains

From natural disasters to geopolitical tensions, and from cyberattacks to economic downturns, the risks that can impact supply chains are numerous and varied. Effective risk management, therefore, involves identifying potential risks, assessing their likelihood and impact, and implementing strategies to mitigate them. This part explores the intricacies of supply chain risk management, providing real-life examples of companies that have successfully navigated the challenges of an unpredictable global environment.

CHAPTER 4   SUPPLY CHAIN INTEGRATION AND COLLABORATION

Understanding Supply Chain Risks

Supply chain risks can be categorized into several types, including operational, financial, strategic, and external risks. Operational risks are those related to the day-to-day functions of the supply chain, such as supplier reliability, transportation issues, or production delays. Financial risks involve factors like currency fluctuations, credit risks, and changes in interest rates. Strategic risks are linked to long-term decisions that can affect the supply chain, such as entering new markets or changing supplier bases. External risks are those beyond the direct control of the company, such as natural disasters, political instability, or regulatory changes.

One of the most illustrative examples of the impact of supply chain risks is the 2011 earthquake and tsunami in Japan. The disaster caused widespread destruction, severely disrupting the supply chains of numerous global companies. One of the hardest-hit sectors was the automotive industry. Toyota, for instance, had to halt production in many of its factories due to shortages of key components, as several of its suppliers were located in the affected regions. The disaster exposed the vulnerabilities in Toyota's supply chain, particularly its reliance on single-source suppliers for critical parts. In response, Toyota revamped its supply chain strategy by diversifying its supplier base and increasing inventory levels for essential components, thereby improving its resilience to future disruptions.

Risk Identification and Assessment

The first step in managing supply chain risks is to identify potential risks and assess their impact. This involves mapping the entire supply chain, from raw material suppliers to end customers, to identify points of vulnerability. Companies often use risk assessment tools, such as failure mode and effects analysis (FMEA) or risk matrices, to evaluate the likelihood of various risks occurring and their potential impact on the business.

A notable example of effective risk identification and assessment is Cisco Systems. In the early 2000s, Cisco faced significant losses due to supply chain disruptions during the dot-com bubble burst. Learning from this experience, Cisco developed a comprehensive risk management framework that includes a Supply Chain Risk Dashboard. This tool allows Cisco to continuously monitor its supply chain for potential risks, such as supplier financial health, geopolitical issues, and natural disasters. By proactively identifying risks, Cisco can implement mitigation strategies before disruptions occur, ensuring the continuity of its operations.

Risk Mitigation Strategies

Once risks have been identified and assessed, companies must develop strategies to mitigate them. These strategies can be preventive, such as diversifying suppliers or increasing inventory levels, or they can be reactive, such as developing contingency plans and setting up crisis management teams.

One company that has successfully implemented risk mitigation strategies is Apple Inc. Known for its complex and tightly controlled supply chain, Apple has taken several steps to minimize risks. For instance, Apple maintains a diversified supplier base, ensuring that no single supplier accounts for a critical percentage of its supply chain. Additionally, Apple invests in long-term contracts with suppliers and even provides financial support to key partners to ensure a stable supply of essential components. Furthermore, Apple keeps strategic inventory reserves for critical components, allowing it to continue production even if a supplier faces disruptions. These measures have enabled Apple to navigate various supply chain challenges, including the COVID-19 pandemic, with minimal impact on its operations.

CHAPTER 4   SUPPLY CHAIN INTEGRATION AND COLLABORATION

The Role of Technology in Supply Chain Risk Management

Technology plays a crucial role in enhancing supply chain risk management. Advanced analytics, artificial intelligence (AI), and blockchain are some of the technologies that companies are leveraging to improve their risk management capabilities.

Advanced analytics and AI, for example, enable companies to predict potential disruptions by analyzing large datasets, such as weather patterns, economic indicators, and social media trends. These technologies can also identify emerging risks that might not be immediately apparent, allowing companies to take preemptive action. For instance, IBM uses AI-powered tools to monitor its global supply chain for potential risks. By analyzing data from various sources, IBM can identify early warning signs of disruptions, such as changes in supplier performance or shifts in market demand. This proactive approach allows IBM to adjust its supply chain strategies in real time, reducing the impact of potential disruptions.

Blockchain technology, on the other hand, provides a transparent and immutable record of transactions across the supply chain. This transparency helps to reduce risks related to fraud, counterfeiting, and compliance. For example, Walmart has implemented a blockchain-based system for tracking the origin of food products in its supply chain. This system not only ensures the authenticity and safety of the products but also enables Walmart to trace the source of any issues quickly, thereby minimizing the risk of widespread recalls.

Building a Resilient Supply Chain

Ultimately, the goal of supply chain risk management is to build a resilient supply chain that can withstand disruptions and recover quickly from setbacks. Resilience is achieved through a combination of proactive risk management strategies, technological innovations, and a culture of continuous improvement.

A prime example of a resilient supply chain is that of Procter & Gamble (P&G). P&G has invested heavily in building flexibility and agility into its supply chain. The company uses a combination of local and global suppliers to ensure a stable supply of raw materials. P&G also employs advanced planning systems that allow it to quickly adjust production schedules in response to changes in demand or supply disruptions. Moreover, P&G has developed strong relationships with its suppliers, based on trust and collaboration, which enable it to work closely with them in times of crisis. This resilience was demonstrated during the COVID-19 pandemic, when P&G was able to maintain the availability of its products, despite significant disruptions in the global supply chain.

The Future of Supply Chain Risk Management

As global supply chains continue to evolve, the importance of effective risk management will only increase. Companies must remain vigilant, continuously monitoring for potential risks and adapting their strategies to address new challenges. The integration of advanced technologies, such as AI and blockchain, will play a critical role in enhancing supply chain risk management capabilities, enabling companies to predict, mitigate, and recover from disruptions more effectively.

However, the key to successful supply chain risk management lies not just in technology but in the ability to foster strong relationships with supply chain partners, build trust, and create a culture of resilience. Companies that can achieve this will be better equipped to navigate the uncertainties of the global business environment, ensuring the continuity of their operations and the satisfaction of their customers.

4.10 Case Studies: Collaborative Supply Chain Success Stories

Successful companies have recognized the need for a more collaborative approach to supply chain management, leading to innovative partnerships, enhanced efficiency, and significant competitive advantages. This portion delves into real-life case studies of companies that have excelled in collaborative supply chain management, showcasing the strategies they employed and the outcomes they achieved.

Case Study 1: Unilever and Its Sustainable Agriculture Initiative

Unilever, one of the world's leading consumer goods companies, has been at the forefront of sustainable supply chain management. Recognizing the importance of sustainable sourcing, Unilever launched its Sustainable Agriculture Initiative (SAI) to collaborate with farmers, suppliers, and other stakeholders. The initiative aims to ensure that agricultural practices meet environmental, social, and economic standards, benefiting all parties involved.

One of the key strategies Unilever employed was the creation of the Unilever Sustainable Agriculture Code (SAC), a set of guidelines that suppliers must adhere to. This code covers various aspects such as soil health, water use, and fair labor practices. Unilever worked closely with suppliers to implement these guidelines, providing training and resources to help them meet the standards.

A significant example of this collaboration is Unilever's partnership with smallholder tea farmers in Kenya. Through the SAI, Unilever has worked with these farmers to improve their agricultural practices, leading to higher yields and better-quality tea. The company provided farmers with access to better seeds, fertilizers, and training on sustainable farming techniques. This collaboration not only helped Unilever secure a sustainable supply of high-quality tea but also improved the livelihoods of the farmers.

The impact of this collaboration has been profound. Unilever's commitment to sustainable sourcing has enhanced its brand reputation, reduced supply chain risks, and contributed to its overall business success. Additionally, the initiative has supported the company's broader goal of making sustainable living commonplace, aligning with consumer expectations for environmentally and socially responsible products. https://www.unilever.com/sustainability/nature/regenerating-nature/.

Case Study 2: Walmart and P&G's Collaborative Planning, Forecasting, and Replenishment (CPFR) Initiative

Walmart and Procter & Gamble (P&G) are two giants in their respective industries, and their collaborative efforts in supply chain management have set a benchmark for others to follow. Their partnership, centered around Collaborative Planning, Forecasting, and Replenishment (CPFR), has transformed the way they manage inventory and meet consumer demand.

CPFR is a process that involves sharing data and forecasts between partners to improve inventory management and reduce stockouts. In the case of Walmart and P&G, the two companies integrated their systems to share real-time data on sales, inventory levels, and forecasts. This collaboration allowed them to synchronize their supply chain activities, ensuring that products were available on Walmart's shelves when consumers wanted them.

A key aspect of this collaboration was the use of shared technology platforms. Walmart and P&G developed a joint forecasting model that took into account various factors such as promotions, seasonal demand, and market trends. By working together on these forecasts, they were able to reduce the bullwhip effect—a common supply chain problem where small fluctuations in demand at the consumer level lead to larger variations in orders at the supplier level.

The results of this collaboration have been impressive. Walmart experienced fewer stockouts, leading to increased sales and customer satisfaction. P&G benefited from more accurate production planning and reduced inventory costs. The success of this partnership has made CPFR a widely adopted practice in the retail industry, demonstrating the power of collaboration in supply chain management. https://www.academia.edu/10317486/How_Walmart_and_P_and_G_Can_Enhance_Supply_Chain_Management_with_CPFR_Initiatives.

Case Study 3: Toyota and Its Just-in-Time (JIT) System with Suppliers

Toyota is renowned for its just-in-time (JIT) production system, a key component of its lean manufacturing philosophy. The success of JIT relies heavily on close collaboration with suppliers to ensure that parts and materials are delivered exactly when they are needed in the production process, without holding excess inventory.

Toyota's approach to supplier collaboration is based on long-term relationships and mutual trust. The company works closely with its suppliers, often providing them with technical support and sharing best practices to improve quality and efficiency. Toyota also engages in joint problem-solving with suppliers, helping them address issues that could impact the supply chain.

A notable example of this collaboration is Toyota's partnership with Denso, one of its key suppliers. Denso and Toyota have worked together for decades, refining the JIT system to achieve remarkable efficiency. Denso delivers parts to Toyota's assembly plants several times a day, in precisely the right quantities needed for production. This close coordination minimizes waste, reduces costs, and ensures that Toyota can respond quickly to changes in consumer demand.

The JIT system, supported by Toyota's collaborative supplier relationships, has been a major factor in the company's success. It has allowed Toyota to maintain high levels of quality, reduce lead times, and remain competitive in a fast-paced automotive market. The Toyota–Denso partnership serves as a prime example of how collaboration can drive supply chain excellence. https://mag.toyota.co.uk/just-in-time/.

Case Study 4: The Coca-Cola Company and Collaborative Logistics with Suppliers

The Coca-Cola Company operates one of the largest and most complex supply chains in the world, with a vast network of bottlers, suppliers, and distributors. To manage this complexity, Coca-Cola has embraced collaborative logistics, working closely with its partners to optimize transportation and distribution processes.

One of the key initiatives Coca-Cola implemented was the establishment of collaborative distribution centers (CDCs). These CDCs serve as shared logistics hubs where multiple suppliers can consolidate their shipments before they are distributed to Coca-Cola's bottling plants. By pooling resources, Coca-Cola and its suppliers are able to achieve economies of scale, reduce transportation costs, and minimize the environmental impact of their operations.

A specific example of this collaboration is Coca-Cola's partnership with C.H. Robinson, a third-party logistics provider. Together, they developed a system for consolidating shipments from multiple suppliers into full truckloads, which are then delivered to Coca-Cola's facilities. This approach not only reduces the number of trucks on the road but also improves delivery times and reduces fuel consumption.

The success of Coca-Cola's collaborative logistics strategy has been significant. The company has achieved cost savings, improved service levels, and reduced its carbon footprint. This collaborative approach to logistics has also strengthened relationships with suppliers, fostering a sense of shared responsibility for the success of the supply chain. https://www.coca-colahellenic.com/en/about-us/what-we-do/supply-chain.

Case Study 5: IBM and Collaborative Innovation in Supply Chain Management

IBM, a global leader in technology and consulting services, has long recognized the value of collaboration in supply chain management. IBM's approach goes beyond traditional supply chain partnerships, focusing on collaborative innovation to drive continuous improvement and stay ahead of market changes.

One of IBM's most successful collaborative initiatives is the integrated supply chain (ISC) program. Through this program, IBM works closely with its suppliers and customers to co-create solutions that enhance supply chain performance. This collaboration involves joint development of new technologies, shared research and development efforts, and open communication channels to address challenges and seize opportunities.

A key example of IBM's collaborative innovation is its partnership with Lenovo, a leading computer manufacturer. When IBM sold its PC division to Lenovo, the two companies established a collaborative supply chain model to ensure a smooth transition and continued success. IBM provided Lenovo with access to its global supply chain network and expertise, while Lenovo shared insights into emerging market trends and consumer preferences. This collaboration enabled Lenovo to rapidly expand its market share and become a dominant player in the global PC industry.

The ISC program has had a profound impact on IBM's supply chain, enabling the company to adapt to changing market conditions, improve efficiency, and deliver innovative solutions to its customers. IBM's collaborative approach to supply chain management has become a model for other companies seeking to leverage partnerships for competitive advantage. https://www.ibm.com/case-studies/ibm-supply-chain.

4.11 The Power of Collaboration in Supply Chain Success

These case studies highlight the transformative power of collaboration in supply chain management. Whether it's through sustainable sourcing, joint forecasting, just-in-time production, collaborative logistics, or innovative partnerships, companies that embrace collaboration are better equipped to navigate the complexities of the global supply chain. By working together with suppliers, customers, and other stakeholders, businesses can achieve greater efficiency, reduce costs, and enhance their ability to respond to market changes. As the global business landscape continues to evolve, the importance of collaboration in supply chain management will only increase, making it a critical factor for success in the years to come.

CHAPTER 5

Future Trends and Innovations in Supply Chain Management

Figure 5-1. *Future Trends and Innovations in Supply Chain Management*

CHAPTER 5   FUTURE TRENDS AND INNOVATIONS IN SUPPLY CHAIN MANAGEMENT

As we move further into the 21st century, several emerging trends and innovations are set to redefine the way supply chains operate. These developments are not just responses to current needs but are proactive strides toward building more resilient, efficient, and sustainable supply chains. In this chapter, we explore the future trends and innovations in supply chain management that are poised to shape the industry in the coming years.

5.1 Digital Supply Chains and the Role of Artificial Intelligence

Digitalization is at the heart of the future supply chain. As companies strive for greater efficiency and accuracy, the adoption of digital technologies is accelerating. Artificial intelligence (AI) and machine learning are leading the charge, offering unprecedented capabilities in data analysis, predictive analytics, and decision-making.

AI-powered tools are increasingly being used to forecast demand, optimize inventory levels, and improve logistics efficiency. For example, companies like Amazon are using AI to predict consumer behavior with remarkable accuracy, allowing for more precise inventory management and faster delivery times. AI can also enhance supply chain visibility by analyzing vast amounts of data from various sources, enabling companies to identify potential disruptions and respond proactively.

Furthermore, the integration of AI with Internet of Things (IoT) devices is creating a new level of connectivity and automation in supply chains. IoT sensors can monitor real-time conditions of goods in transit, while AI algorithms analyze this data to optimize routing, reduce energy consumption, and ensure timely delivery. This digital transformation is not only enhancing operational efficiency but also enabling companies to offer more personalized services to their customers.

CHAPTER 5   FUTURE TRENDS AND INNOVATIONS IN SUPPLY CHAIN MANAGEMENT

5.2 Blockchain Technology for Enhanced Transparency and Security

Blockchain technology, initially developed as the backbone of cryptocurrencies, is now being recognized for its potential to revolutionize supply chain management. Blockchain's decentralized and immutable ledger system offers a high level of transparency and security, which are critical for managing complex global supply chains.

One of the key benefits of blockchain in supply chain management is its ability to provide end-to-end traceability. Every transaction or movement of goods can be recorded on a blockchain, creating a tamper-proof audit trail. This is particularly valuable in industries like food and pharmaceuticals, where consumers and regulators demand proof of origin and quality. For instance, Walmart has implemented blockchain technology to trace the origin of its fresh produce, reducing the time it takes to track a product from days to seconds.

Blockchain also enhances security by reducing the risk of fraud and counterfeiting. Smart contracts, which are self-executing contracts with the terms of the agreement directly written into code, can automate and enforce contract terms, ensuring that all parties comply with their obligations. This not only streamlines processes but also reduces the need for intermediaries, lowering costs and increasing efficiency.

5.3 Sustainable Supply Chain Practices

Sustainability is no longer a buzzword; it is a critical business imperative. Companies are increasingly recognizing that sustainable supply chain practices are essential for long-term success. This shift is driven by growing consumer awareness, regulatory pressures, and the need to mitigate environmental risks.

CHAPTER 5   FUTURE TRENDS AND INNOVATIONS IN SUPPLY CHAIN MANAGEMENT

One of the most significant trends in this area is the adoption of circular economy principles. In a circular economy, resources are kept in use for as long as possible, products are designed for longevity, and waste is minimized through recycling and reuse. For example, companies like Nike and H&M are embracing circular supply chains by designing products that can be easily disassembled and recycled at the end of their life cycle.

Another important trend is the use of renewable energy in supply chain operations. Companies are increasingly investing in solar, wind, and other renewable energy sources to power their manufacturing and logistics operations. This not only reduces their carbon footprint but also helps them manage energy costs more effectively. Additionally, sustainable packaging solutions, such as biodegradable materials and reusable containers, are gaining traction as companies seek to reduce their environmental impact.

5.4 The Rise of E-commerce and Omnichannel Supply Chains

The rapid growth of e-commerce has fundamentally changed the dynamics of supply chain management. Consumers today expect fast, convenient, and flexible delivery options, which has led to the rise of omnichannel supply chains. In an omnichannel supply chain, products are sourced, stored, and delivered across multiple channels, including online platforms, brick-and-mortar stores, and mobile apps.

To meet these demands, companies are rethinking their distribution strategies and investing in technologies that enable real-time inventory visibility and agile fulfillment. For instance, the use of distributed warehouses and micro-fulfillment centers is becoming more common, allowing companies to position inventory closer to the end consumer and reduce delivery times. Retail giants like Walmart and Target have successfully implemented omnichannel strategies, offering services like buy online, pick up in-store (BOPIS), and same-day delivery to enhance the customer experience.

The integration of advanced analytics and AI is also playing a crucial role in optimizing omnichannel supply chains. By analyzing consumer data across different channels, companies can better understand buying patterns and preferences, enabling them to tailor their inventory and distribution strategies accordingly. This level of customization not only improves customer satisfaction but also drives operational efficiency.

5.5 Resilient and Agile Supply Chains

The COVID-19 pandemic highlighted the vulnerabilities of global supply chains, prompting companies to prioritize resilience and agility. Moving forward, supply chains will need to be more adaptable to disruptions, whether they stem from natural disasters, geopolitical tensions, or unexpected demand fluctuations.

One of the key strategies for building resilient supply chains is diversification. Companies are moving away from single-source suppliers and, instead, adopting multisourcing strategies to mitigate the risk of supply disruptions. Additionally, regionalization is becoming more prevalent as companies seek to shorten supply chains and reduce dependence on distant suppliers. This shift toward regional supply chains not only enhances resilience but also supports sustainability goals by reducing transportation emissions.

Agility is another critical factor in future supply chains. Companies are increasingly adopting just-in-case inventory strategies, maintaining higher buffer stocks to respond quickly to sudden changes in demand. The use of advanced planning and forecasting tools is also on the rise, enabling companies to anticipate disruptions and adjust their supply chain operations accordingly.

Moreover, digital twins—virtual replicas of physical supply chains—are emerging as a powerful tool for enhancing resilience. By simulating different scenarios and stress-testing their supply chains, companies can identify potential vulnerabilities and develop contingency plans. This proactive approach to risk management is crucial for navigating the uncertainties of the future.

5.6 Embracing the Future of Supply Chain Management

The future of supply chain management is being shaped by a combination of digital innovation, sustainability, and the need for greater resilience. As companies navigate the complexities of a rapidly changing global landscape, those that embrace these trends and invest in the necessary technologies will be better positioned to thrive. The integration of AI, blockchain, and sustainable practices, coupled with the agility to respond to disruptions, will be key to building supply chains that are not only efficient and cost-effective but also resilient and responsible. As we look ahead, the ongoing evolution of supply chain management will continue to unlock new opportunities for innovation and collaboration, driving the industry toward a more sustainable and interconnected future.

5.7 The Impact of Artificial Intelligence and Machine Learning

Artificial intelligence (AI) and machine learning (ML) have emerged as transformative technologies in supply chain management, fundamentally altering how businesses operate, compete, and grow. The infusion of AI and ML into supply chain processes has unlocked unprecedented levels of efficiency, agility, and responsiveness, enabling companies to adapt to ever-changing market conditions, manage risks more effectively, and deliver superior customer experiences. This chapter delves into the

CHAPTER 5   FUTURE TRENDS AND INNOVATIONS IN SUPPLY CHAIN MANAGEMENT

impact of AI and ML on supply chain management, highlighting their applications, benefits, and real-life examples of companies leveraging these technologies to gain a competitive edge.

Enhanced Demand Forecasting and Inventory Management

One of the most significant impacts of AI and ML in supply chain management is in demand forecasting and inventory management. Traditional methods of demand forecasting relied heavily on historical sales data and simple statistical models, which often led to inaccuracies due to their inability to account for complex variables such as seasonality, market trends, and consumer behavior shifts. AI and ML, however, utilize vast amounts of data from various sources—including social media, weather patterns, economic indicators, and even competitors' activities—to create more accurate demand forecasts.

A prime example of this is Unilever, which has successfully implemented AI-driven demand forecasting tools across its global supply chain. By integrating ML algorithms into its forecasting process, Unilever can analyze millions of data points in real time, leading to more accurate predictions of consumer demand. This has resulted in a significant reduction in inventory levels and improved product availability, ultimately enhancing customer satisfaction and reducing costs associated with excess inventory and stockouts.

Optimized Logistics and Transportation

Logistics and transportation are other areas where AI and ML are making a profound impact. AI-powered solutions can optimize routes, reduce fuel consumption, and minimize delivery times by analyzing real-time traffic data, weather conditions, and historical transportation patterns. These technologies also enable predictive maintenance of fleet vehicles, reducing downtime and preventing costly breakdowns.

DHL, a global logistics leader, has been at the forefront of leveraging AI and ML to optimize its logistics operations. The company uses AI algorithms to analyze data from its vast network of vehicles and delivery routes to identify the most efficient paths and delivery schedules. This approach has reduced delivery times and lowered operational costs, enhancing overall service quality. Additionally, DHL employs predictive analytics to forecast potential disruptions, such as adverse weather conditions or traffic congestion, allowing them to make proactive adjustments to their logistics plans.

Automated Quality Control and Defect Detection

In manufacturing and production, AI and ML are revolutionizing quality control processes by enabling automated defect detection and quality assurance. Traditional quality control methods often involve manual inspection, which is time-consuming, error-prone, and costly. AI-driven vision systems, combined with ML algorithms, can rapidly analyze visual data from production lines, identifying defects and inconsistencies in real time with a higher accuracy rate than human inspectors.

Siemens, a leading technology company, has implemented AI-based quality control systems in its electronic manufacturing plants. These systems use computer vision and deep learning algorithms to inspect electronic components for defects as they move through the production line. The AI system can detect minute flaws that are often missed by human inspectors, leading to a significant reduction in defective products and an overall improvement in product quality. This not only reduces waste but also enhances customer satisfaction and brand reputation.

Supply Chain Risk Management and Resilience Building

AI and ML are also playing a critical role in supply chain risk management and building resilience against disruptions. The COVID-19 pandemic highlighted the vulnerabilities of global supply chains and underscored the need for robust risk management strategies. AI and ML tools can predict potential disruptions by analyzing a wide range of risk factors, including geopolitical events, natural disasters, and supplier reliability. This allows companies to develop contingency plans and mitigate risks more effectively.

IBM, for instance, has developed an AI-based risk management platform known as IBM Supply Chain Intelligence Suite. This platform uses AI algorithms to monitor global supply chain activities and detect early warning signs of potential disruptions. By analyzing data from multiple sources, such as news feeds, social media, and financial reports, the platform provides real-time insights and actionable recommendations for mitigating risks. This proactive approach to risk management enables companies to respond quickly to unexpected events, minimizing their impact on supply chain operations.

Enhanced Supplier Relationship Management

Supplier relationship management is another area where AI and ML are making a substantial impact. AI-driven platforms can analyze vast amounts of data related to supplier performance, pricing, delivery times, and quality metrics to provide deeper insights into supplier reliability and efficiency. This allows companies to identify the best suppliers, negotiate better terms, and foster stronger relationships.

Coupa, a leading provider of business spend management solutions, has integrated AI and ML into its supplier management platform. The platform uses AI algorithms to assess supplier risk by analyzing various factors, such as financial stability, delivery performance, and compliance with regulatory requirements. This enables companies to make more informed decisions when selecting suppliers, reducing the risk of supply chain disruptions and ensuring a more reliable supply of goods and services.

Personalized Customer Experiences and Demand Shaping

AI and ML are also being used to enhance customer experiences by enabling personalized and demand-shaping strategies. By analyzing customer data, such as purchase history, browsing behavior, and social media interactions, AI algorithms can identify individual preferences and tailor marketing and sales strategies accordingly. This allows companies to offer personalized product recommendations, promotions, and pricing strategies that align with customer needs and preferences.

Starbucks has leveraged AI and ML to create personalized customer experiences through its mobile app and loyalty program. The company uses ML algorithms to analyze customer data and provide personalized drink recommendations, offers, and promotions. This data-driven approach has resulted in higher customer engagement and loyalty, driving increased sales and revenue growth.

Ethical AI and Sustainable Supply Chain Practices

As AI and ML become more integrated into supply chain management, there is a growing emphasis on ethical AI and sustainable supply chain practices. Companies are increasingly aware of the need to ensure that AI algorithms are transparent, fair, and free from bias. Additionally, there is a push toward using AI to promote sustainability in supply chain operations, such as reducing carbon emissions, minimizing waste, and promoting ethical sourcing.

Microsoft has taken significant steps to ensure that its AI initiatives align with ethical standards and sustainability goals. The company has implemented a responsible AI framework that guides the development and deployment of AI technologies in its supply chain operations. Microsoft is also using AI to optimize its supply chain for sustainability, such as reducing energy consumption in its data centers and promoting circular economy practices by recycling and reusing electronic components.

The Future of AI and ML in Supply Chain Management

AI and ML are no longer just buzzwords; they are powerful tools that are reshaping the future of supply chain management. From enhancing demand forecasting and optimizing logistics to improving quality control and managing risks, these technologies are unlocking new levels of efficiency, agility, and resilience. As companies continue to navigate the complexities of the global supply chain landscape, those that leverage AI and ML will be better positioned to stay ahead of the curve, deliver superior customer experiences, and achieve sustainable growth.

5.8 Blockchain Technology in Supply Chains

Blockchain technology has emerged as a transformative force across various industries, and supply chain management is no exception. Originally conceptualized as the foundation for cryptocurrencies like Bitcoin, blockchain's unique capabilities—such as decentralization, transparency, immutability, and security—make it an ideal tool for enhancing supply chain operations. This section explores how blockchain technology is revolutionizing supply chain management, providing detailed insights into its applications, benefits, and examples of companies leveraging blockchain to create more efficient, transparent, and secure supply chains.

Understanding Blockchain Technology in Supply Chains

At its core, blockchain is a distributed ledger technology (DLT) that records transactions in a secure, transparent, and tamper-proof manner. Each "block" in a blockchain contains a record of transactions, and these blocks are linked together in a "chain" using cryptographic hashes. Because each block is connected to the previous one and contains a timestamp, altering any transaction within a block would require changing all subsequent blocks, making fraud nearly impossible.

In supply chain management, blockchain provides an immutable record of every transaction that takes place along the supply chain, from raw material sourcing to manufacturing, shipping, and final delivery to the customer. This level of transparency ensures that all stakeholders—including suppliers, manufacturers, distributors, and customers—have access to a single, unalterable version of the truth, reducing disputes, enhancing trust, and streamlining operations.

CHAPTER 5   FUTURE TRENDS AND INNOVATIONS IN SUPPLY CHAIN MANAGEMENT

Enhancing Traceability and Transparency

One of the most significant benefits of blockchain technology in supply chains is enhanced traceability and transparency. With consumers increasingly demanding more information about the origins and journey of the products they purchase, companies are under pressure to provide detailed visibility into their supply chains. Blockchain technology enables this by providing a transparent and immutable ledger of all transactions, ensuring that every step of a product's journey is recorded and can be verified.

Example: Walmart and Food Safety
Walmart has implemented blockchain technology to improve food safety and traceability in its supply chain. By partnering with IBM and using the IBM Food Trust blockchain platform, Walmart can trace the origin of food products, such as leafy greens, back to their source in seconds rather than days. This rapid traceability has been instrumental in quickly identifying and isolating contaminated products during foodborne illness outbreaks, minimizing the impact on consumers and reducing waste. For instance, during the *E. coli* outbreak linked to romaine lettuce, Walmart's blockchain system enabled them to trace the affected products quickly and remove them from their shelves, enhancing consumer safety and trust. https://tech.walmart.com/content/walmart-global-tech/en_us/blog/post/blockchain-in-the-food-supply-chain.html#:~:text=Walmart%2C%20along%20with%20JD%2C%20IBM,consortium%20to%20enhance%20food%20safety.

Improving Supply Chain Efficiency and Reducing Costs

Blockchain technology also offers significant potential for improving supply chain efficiency and reducing costs. By providing a single, immutable ledger accessible to all supply chain participants, blockchain eliminates the need for multiple, siloed databases and reduces the

CHAPTER 5   FUTURE TRENDS AND INNOVATIONS IN SUPPLY CHAIN MANAGEMENT

reliance on intermediaries for transaction verification. This streamlining of processes can lead to faster transaction times, reduced administrative costs, and lower risks of errors and fraud.

Example: De Beers and Diamond Supply Chain
De Beers, the world's leading diamond company, has implemented blockchain technology to streamline its diamond supply chain and enhance transparency. The company's Tracr platform uses blockchain to track diamonds from the mine to the retail store, ensuring that each diamond is conflict-free and ethically sourced. By digitizing the diamond's journey on a secure blockchain ledger, De Beers has been able to reduce paperwork, minimize the risk of fraud, and provide customers with a verifiable guarantee of a diamond's authenticity and ethical origins. This increased transparency and efficiency have reduced operational costs and strengthened De Beers' brand reputation. `https://www.debeersgroup.com/~/media/Files/D/De-Beers-Group/documents/building-forever/diamond-dialogues-de-deers-and-the-sdgspdf.pdf`.

Combating Counterfeiting and Ensuring Product Authenticity

Counterfeiting and fraud pose significant challenges for many industries, particularly in sectors like pharmaceuticals, luxury goods, and electronics. Blockchain technology provides a robust solution to these challenges by creating an immutable and transparent record of a product's journey through the supply chain. This makes it nearly impossible for counterfeit goods to be introduced into the supply chain without detection.

Example: Pfizer and the Pharmaceutical Industry
Pfizer, a global leader in the pharmaceutical industry, is leveraging blockchain technology to combat counterfeiting and ensure the authenticity of its medicines. By implementing a blockchain-based system, Pfizer can track each batch of medicine from production to distribution, creating a secure and verifiable record of its journey. This

traceability is crucial in preventing counterfeit drugs from entering the supply chain, protecting patient safety, and maintaining regulatory compliance. Blockchain technology also enables seamless verification of product authenticity by healthcare providers and pharmacies, enhancing trust and transparency across the pharmaceutical supply chain. https://www.pfizer.com/.

Facilitating Smart Contracts and Automating Transactions

Blockchain technology also enables the use of smart contracts—self-executing contracts with the terms of the agreement directly written into code. Smart contracts can automatically trigger actions when predefined conditions are met, such as releasing payment once goods are delivered and inspected. This automation reduces the need for intermediaries, minimizes delays, and ensures that all parties uphold their contractual obligations.

Example: Maersk and Shipping Logistics
Maersk, the global shipping giant, has partnered with IBM to develop TradeLens, a blockchain-based platform for the shipping industry. TradeLens uses smart contracts to automate various aspects of shipping logistics, such as customs clearance and freight payment. By digitizing and automating these processes, TradeLens has significantly reduced paperwork, minimized delays, and improved the overall efficiency of global shipping operations. For instance, Maersk reported a 40% reduction in transit times for certain shipments due to the streamlined processes enabled by blockchain technology. This not only reduces costs but also improves customer satisfaction by providing more reliable and timely deliveries. https://www.prnewswire.com/news-releases/maersk-and-ibm-introduce-tradelens-blockchain-shipping-solution-300694642.html.

Enhancing Supplier Relationship Management and Collaboration

Blockchain technology also plays a crucial role in enhancing supplier relationship management and fostering collaboration across the supply chain. By providing a transparent and secure platform for sharing information, blockchain enables companies to build stronger, more collaborative relationships with their suppliers. This transparency helps to align incentives, improve communication, and foster trust among all supply chain participants.

Example: Unilever and Sustainable Sourcing
Unilever, a multinational consumer goods company, has implemented blockchain technology to enhance transparency and collaboration in its palm oil supply chain. By using blockchain, Unilever can trace the journey of palm oil from the plantation to the final product, ensuring that it is sustainably sourced and meets ethical standards. This transparency enables Unilever to work more closely with its suppliers, promoting sustainable practices and improving overall supply chain performance. Moreover, by sharing data on blockchain, Unilever has been able to engage more effectively with stakeholders, including NGOs and consumers, enhancing its reputation as a leader in sustainability.

Addressing Regulatory Compliance and Sustainability Goals

Blockchain technology also supports companies in meeting regulatory compliance and sustainability goals by providing a transparent and verifiable record of supply chain activities. This is particularly important in industries where compliance with environmental, social, and governance (ESG) standards is critical. Blockchain technology enables companies to demonstrate compliance with regulations and sustainability commitments, enhancing their reputation and reducing the risk of fines and penalties.

CHAPTER 5   FUTURE TRENDS AND INNOVATIONS IN SUPPLY CHAIN MANAGEMENT

Example: Renault and Automotive Compliance

Renault, a leading automotive manufacturer, has leveraged blockchain technology to enhance compliance and sustainability in its supply chain. The company has developed a blockchain-based system to track the entire life cycle of its vehicles, from production to end-of-life recycling. This system provides a transparent and auditable record of the materials used in each vehicle, ensuring compliance with environmental regulations and promoting sustainable practices. By using blockchain to track and verify its supply chain activities, Renault can demonstrate its commitment to sustainability and regulatory compliance, enhancing its brand reputation and reducing risks associated with noncompliance. `https://media.renaultgroup.com/groupe-renault-tested-a-blockchain-project-to-go-further-in-the-certification-of-vehicle-compliance/`.

The Future of Blockchain in Supply Chain Management

Blockchain technology is rapidly becoming a game-changer in supply chain management, offering numerous benefits ranging from enhanced transparency and traceability to improved efficiency and reduced costs. As companies continue to navigate the complexities of global supply chains, those that embrace blockchain technology will be better positioned to build resilient, secure, and sustainable supply chains capable of thriving in an increasingly dynamic and competitive landscape.

5.9 The Role of Big Data and Analytics

Big data analytics involves the use of advanced algorithms and tools to extract meaningful insights from vast and complex datasets, enabling supply chain professionals to make more informed decisions, predict future trends, and respond proactively to changing market conditions.

CHAPTER 5 FUTURE TRENDS AND INNOVATIONS IN SUPPLY CHAIN MANAGEMENT

This part explores the transformative impact of big data and analytics on supply chain management, providing a detailed overview of its applications, benefits, and real-life examples of companies leveraging these technologies to achieve superior performance.

Understanding Big Data in Supply Chains

Big data in supply chain management refers to the massive volumes of structured and unstructured data generated from various sources, including sensors, RFID tags, GPS systems, social media, transactional systems, and customer interactions. The sheer volume, velocity, variety, and veracity of this data make traditional data processing methods inadequate. Big data analytics leverages advanced technologies such as machine learning, artificial intelligence, and cloud computing to analyze this data in real time, uncovering hidden patterns, correlations, and insights that can drive better decision-making and operational efficiency.

In supply chain management, big data analytics can be applied across various functions, including demand forecasting, inventory management, procurement, transportation, and customer service. By analyzing data from these diverse sources, companies can gain a holistic view of their supply chain, identify inefficiencies, predict disruptions, and optimize their operations to achieve cost savings and improved service levels.

Enhancing Demand Forecasting and Inventory Optimization

One of the most significant applications of big data analytics in supply chain management is in enhancing demand forecasting and inventory optimization. Accurate demand forecasting is crucial for maintaining the right balance between supply and demand, minimizing stockouts, reducing excess inventory, and improving customer satisfaction.

Traditional forecasting methods often rely on historical sales data and fail to account for the complexities of modern supply chains, such as seasonality, promotions, market trends, and external factors like economic conditions and weather patterns.

Example: Zara's Data-Driven Approach to Inventory Management
Zara, the global fashion retailer, has successfully leveraged big data analytics to optimize its inventory management and improve its demand forecasting capabilities. By analyzing data from multiple sources, including point-of-sale systems, social media, and customer feedback, Zara can predict fashion trends and adjust its production and inventory levels accordingly. This data-driven approach enables Zara to respond quickly to changing customer preferences, reduce lead times, and minimize excess inventory, resulting in higher sales and reduced markdowns. By using big data analytics to optimize its inventory management, Zara has been able to maintain its position as a leader in the fast-fashion industry. `https://medium.com/thedeephub/zaras-fashion-revolution-through-data-insights-28f8fa728a0f#:~:text=Zara's%20data%2Ddriven%20approach%20extends,business%2C%20from%20storefronts%20to%20websites.`

Improving Supplier Relationship Management and Procurement

Big data analytics also plays a crucial role in improving supplier relationship management and procurement processes. By analyzing data from supplier transactions, performance metrics, market trends, and external factors, companies can gain deeper insights into supplier behavior, identify risks and opportunities, and negotiate better contracts. Big data analytics enables supply chain professionals to assess supplier performance more accurately, predict potential disruptions, and develop more effective supplier management strategies.

Example: Procter & Gamble's Data-Driven Supplier Collaboration
Procter & Gamble (P&G), a leading consumer goods company, has implemented a big data analytics platform to enhance its supplier collaboration and procurement processes. By integrating data from its global supply chain network, P&G can analyze supplier performance, assess risks, and identify opportunities for improvement. This data-driven approach has enabled P&G to negotiate better contracts, reduce procurement costs, and build stronger relationships with its suppliers. For example, P&G's analytics platform helps the company identify suppliers that consistently deliver high-quality materials on time, allowing it to prioritize these suppliers and develop long-term partnerships. This improved supplier collaboration has contributed to P&G's ability to maintain high product quality and reliability in the market. `https://www.forbes.com/sites/noahbarsky/2021/10/26/procter-gamble-tech-spending-boosts-supply-chain-resilience/`.

Enhancing Transportation and Logistics Optimization

Transportation and logistics are critical components of supply chain management, and big data analytics has the potential to revolutionize these functions by providing real-time visibility, optimizing routes, and reducing costs. By analyzing data from GPS systems, telematics, weather forecasts, traffic patterns, and fuel prices, companies can optimize their transportation routes, minimize delays, reduce fuel consumption, and improve overall efficiency.

Example: UPS's ORION System for Route Optimization
United Parcel Service (UPS), a global leader in logistics and transportation, has developed a sophisticated big data analytics platform called ORION (On-Road Integrated Optimization and Navigation) to optimize its delivery routes and improve operational efficiency. ORION uses advanced

CHAPTER 5   FUTURE TRENDS AND INNOVATIONS IN SUPPLY CHAIN MANAGEMENT

algorithms to analyze data from various sources, including GPS, traffic patterns, and delivery schedules, to determine the most efficient routes for its drivers. By optimizing routes, ORION has enabled UPS to reduce fuel consumption, lower emissions, and improve delivery times. For example, ORION has helped UPS save millions of gallons of fuel annually and reduce CO_2 emissions by thousands of metric tons, contributing to the company's sustainability goals and improving its bottom line. https://about.ups.com/us/en/newsroom/press-releases/innovation-driven/ups-to-enhance-orion-with-continuous-delivery-route-optimization.html.

Enhancing Risk Management and Resilience

In today's volatile and uncertain business environment, effective risk management and resilience are critical for supply chain success. Big data analytics provides supply chain professionals with the tools they need to identify potential risks, predict disruptions, and develop proactive mitigation strategies. By analyzing data from various sources, including weather forecasts, geopolitical events, and supplier performance, companies can gain real-time insights into potential risks and take corrective actions before disruptions occur.

Example: IBM's Risk Management Platform for Supply Chain Resilience
IBM, a global technology leader, has developed a big data analytics platform called IBM Sterling Supply Chain Insights with Watson to enhance supply chain risk management and resilience. The platform uses artificial intelligence and machine learning algorithms to analyze data from various sources, including news feeds, social media, and IoT sensors, to identify potential risks and disruptions in the supply chain. For instance, the platform can detect weather-related risks, such as hurricanes or floods, that could impact transportation routes and proactively suggest alternative

routes or suppliers. By providing real-time insights and predictive analytics, IBM's platform enables companies to respond more quickly to disruptions, reduce downtime, and maintain continuity of operations. https://www.ibm.com/topics/supply-chain-risk-management.

Driving Customer-Centric Supply Chains

Big data analytics also plays a critical role in driving customer-centric supply chains by enabling companies to better understand customer preferences, predict demand, and personalize their offerings. By analyzing customer data from multiple touchpoints, including e-commerce platforms, social media, and customer service interactions, companies can gain valuable insights into customer behavior and preferences, allowing them to tailor their products and services to meet customer needs.

Example: Amazon's Personalized Customer Experience
Amazon, the world's largest online retailer, has mastered the use of big data analytics to create a highly personalized customer experience. By analyzing data from customer interactions, purchase history, browsing behavior, and social media, Amazon can predict customer preferences and offer personalized product recommendations. This data-driven approach has enabled Amazon to enhance customer satisfaction, increase sales, and build customer loyalty. For example, Amazon's recommendation engine, powered by big data analytics, accounts for a significant portion of its sales by suggesting products that customers are likely to purchase based on their previous behavior. This personalized approach has been a key factor in Amazon's success and dominance in the e-commerce market. https://aws.amazon.com/personalize/.

CHAPTER 5   FUTURE TRENDS AND INNOVATIONS IN SUPPLY CHAIN MANAGEMENT

Leveraging Predictive and Prescriptive Analytics for Strategic Decision-Making

Predictive and prescriptive analytics are advanced forms of big data analytics that enable supply chain professionals to anticipate future trends and make strategic decisions based on data-driven insights. Predictive analytics uses historical data and machine learning algorithms to forecast future events, such as demand fluctuations or supplier performance issues, while prescriptive analytics provides recommendations on the best course of action based on these predictions.

Example: DHL's Predictive Analytics for Demand Forecasting
DHL, a global leader in logistics and supply chain management, has implemented predictive analytics to enhance its demand forecasting capabilities and improve its strategic decision-making. By analyzing historical shipment data, market trends, and external factors, DHL's predictive analytics platform can forecast future demand for its logistics services with high accuracy. This enables DHL to optimize its workforce planning, fleet management, and inventory levels, ensuring that it can meet customer demand efficiently and cost-effectively. For example, during peak seasons, such as the holiday shopping period, DHL uses predictive analytics to anticipate spikes in demand and adjust its operations accordingly, ensuring timely deliveries and high customer satisfaction. `https://www.dhl.com/global-en/delivered/innovation/big-data-analytics-in-supply-chain-management.html`.

The Future of Big Data and Analytics in Supply Chain Management

Big data and analytics are revolutionizing supply chain management by providing unprecedented visibility, agility, and efficiency across the entire supply chain. As companies continue to navigate the complexities of global supply chains, those that embrace big data analytics will be better positioned to anticipate changes, optimize operations, and create value for their customers. The future of supply chain management lies in the intelligent use of data and analytics to drive innovation, enhance resilience, and build more customer-centric supply chains capable of thriving in a rapidly evolving business landscape.

5.10 Sustainable Supply Chain Practices

Companies today face increasing pressure from stakeholders—ranging from customers and investors to regulators and nongovernmental organizations—to operate responsibly and sustainably. This shift necessitates that supply chains, which encompass everything from sourcing raw materials to delivering finished products to customers, become more transparent, efficient, and environmentally friendly.

The Importance of Sustainability in Supply Chains

Sustainability in supply chain management involves integrating environmental and social considerations into every stage of the supply chain process. This approach seeks to minimize negative impacts on the environment and society while maximizing economic benefits. The importance of sustainable supply chains is underscored by several factors:

- **Regulatory Compliance:** Governments worldwide are introducing stricter environmental regulations. Companies must ensure their supply chains comply with these rules to avoid legal penalties and reputational damage.

- **Consumer Demand:** Today's consumers are more environmentally conscious and demand transparency about the products they buy. Brands perceived as sustainable often enjoy higher customer loyalty and brand equity.

- **Cost Savings:** Sustainable practices, such as reducing waste and improving energy efficiency, can lead to significant cost savings.

- **Risk Management:** Sustainable supply chains are more resilient to disruptions caused by climate change, resource scarcity, and geopolitical events.

Given these factors, companies are increasingly prioritizing sustainability as a key objective in their supply chain strategies.

Key Components of Sustainable Supply Chain Practices

To build a sustainable supply chain, companies need to focus on several key areas:

- **Sustainable Sourcing:** Ensuring that raw materials and products are sourced ethically and sustainably. This involves working with suppliers who adhere to environmental and social standards.

- **Energy Efficiency:** Reducing energy consumption in manufacturing, transportation, and distribution processes to lower carbon footprints.

- **Waste Management:** Implementing practices to reduce, reuse, and recycle waste materials across the supply chain.

- **Green Logistics:** Optimizing transportation routes, using fuel-efficient vehicles, and employing eco-friendly packaging materials.

- **Social Responsibility:** Ensuring fair labor practices, supporting local communities, and enhancing workforce diversity and inclusion throughout the supply chain.

These components not only help reduce environmental impacts but also improve operational efficiency and foster a positive corporate image.

Examples of Sustainable Supply Chain Practices

Example 1: Unilever's Sustainable Living Plan

Unilever, a global leader in consumer goods, has been at the forefront of sustainability with its "Sustainable Living Plan." The company aims to halve its environmental footprint while increasing its positive social impact. A critical component of this plan is Unilever's commitment to sourcing 100% of its agricultural raw materials sustainably. To achieve this, Unilever works closely with suppliers to promote sustainable farming practices, reduce water usage, and minimize the use of harmful pesticides and fertilizers.

Unilever has partnered with Rainforest Alliance and Fairtrade to ensure that its tea suppliers in Kenya, India, and other regions adhere to sustainable farming practices. By doing so, Unilever not only supports local communities by paying fair wages but also promotes biodiversity and reduces deforestation. This approach has helped Unilever achieve a 31% reduction in greenhouse gas emissions per ton of production since 2010, demonstrating how sustainable supply chain practices can lead to tangible environmental benefits.

Example 2: Patagonia's Commitment to Environmental Responsibility

Patagonia, an outdoor apparel company, is renowned for its commitment to environmental responsibility. The company's supply chain strategy focuses on sustainability at every stage, from product design to manufacturing and recycling. Patagonia uses only organic cotton, recycled polyester, and other sustainable materials in its products. The company also works with suppliers to ensure that their manufacturing processes are environmentally friendly and that workers are treated fairly.

One notable initiative is Patagonia's "Worn Wear" program, which encourages customers to repair, reuse, and recycle their clothing. By promoting product longevity and reducing waste, Patagonia has created a circular supply chain model that minimizes environmental impact. In addition, Patagonia's supply chain transparency initiative allows customers to trace the origins of their products, fostering greater accountability and trust. `https://www.patagonia.com/our-responsibility-programs.html`.

Example 3: IKEA's Circular Supply Chain Model

IKEA, the world's largest furniture retailer, has embraced a circular supply chain model as part of its sustainability strategy. The company aims to become a "climate positive" business by 2030, meaning it will reduce more greenhouse gas emissions than its entire value chain emits. To achieve this, IKEA is rethinking its product design, sourcing, manufacturing, and end-of-life management.

One key aspect of IKEA's approach is its commitment to using only renewable and recycled materials in its products. For example, IKEA has introduced a new line of furniture made entirely from recycled plastic and wood. Additionally, IKEA encourages customers to return their old furniture for recycling or resale, creating a closed-loop system that reduces waste and extends the life cycle of its products.

IKEA also works closely with suppliers to implement sustainable forestry practices and reduce water usage in production processes. By promoting a circular economy, IKEA not only minimizes its environmental impact but also creates new business opportunities and strengthens its brand reputation as a leader in sustainability. https://www.ikea.com/ global/en/our-business/sustainability/our-circular-agenda/.

The Challenges of Implementing Sustainable Supply Chain Practices

Despite the numerous benefits, implementing sustainable supply chain practices is not without challenges. Companies may face several obstacles, including

- **High Initial Costs:** Transitioning to sustainable practices often requires significant upfront investments in new technologies, infrastructure, and training.

- **Complexity and Lack of Transparency:** Supply chains are often complex and involve multiple tiers of suppliers, making it challenging to monitor and enforce sustainability standards.

- **Resistance to Change:** Some suppliers and internal stakeholders may resist changes to established practices, especially if they perceive sustainability initiatives as costly or time-consuming.

- **Balancing Sustainability with Profitability:** Companies must find a balance between achieving sustainability goals and maintaining profitability, particularly in highly competitive industries.

To overcome these challenges, companies are fostering a culture of sustainability, invest in the necessary resources, and work collaboratively with suppliers and other stakeholders to achieve their goals.

The Future of Sustainable Supply Chains

As global environmental concerns continue to rise, the importance of sustainable supply chains will only grow. Companies that proactively adopt sustainable practices will be better positioned to thrive in a rapidly evolving market landscape. Emerging trends in sustainable supply chain management include

- **Increased Use of Technology:** Technologies such as blockchain, IoT, and AI are being increasingly used to enhance supply chain transparency, traceability, and efficiency.

- **Greater Collaboration:** Companies are forming strategic partnerships with suppliers, NGOs, and other stakeholders to achieve sustainability goals more effectively.

- **Focus on Circular Economy:** The shift from a linear "take-make-dispose" model to a circular economy, where products are designed for reuse, recycling, and regeneration, is becoming more prominent.

- **Emphasis on Social Sustainability:** Beyond environmental considerations, companies are also focusing on social sustainability by ensuring fair labor practices, supporting local communities, and enhancing workforce diversity.

Sustainable supply chain practices are not just a trend but a necessity for businesses looking to build long-term resilience, enhance brand reputation, and contribute to a more sustainable future. Companies that successfully integrate sustainability into their supply chains can achieve significant environmental, social, and economic benefits, positioning themselves as leaders in their industries.

5.11 The Future of E-commerce and Omnichannel Logistics

The future of e-commerce and omnichannel logistics will be defined by advanced technologies, innovative strategies, and a customer-centric approach that prioritizes convenience, speed, and personalization. This section explores the key trends and innovations shaping the future of e-commerce and omnichannel logistics, highlighting how businesses can stay ahead in this competitive environment.

The Evolution of E-commerce and Consumer Expectations

E-commerce has undergone significant changes over the past decade, transitioning from a supplementary sales channel to a primary revenue driver for many businesses. The COVID-19 pandemic accelerated this shift, pushing consumers to embrace online shopping for everything from groceries to luxury goods. This change in behavior has led to heightened expectations around delivery speed, product availability, and the overall shopping experience.

Consumers now demand more than just fast delivery; they want flexibility in how and where they receive their orders. This expectation has fueled the rise of omnichannel logistics—a strategy that integrates multiple sales and distribution channels to provide a unified customer experience. Whether shopping online, via mobile apps, or in brick-and-mortar stores, customers expect a seamless, personalized journey. Businesses that can deliver this integrated experience are well-positioned to capture and retain market share in the future.

Key Drivers of Omnichannel Logistics

Several factors are driving the growth and evolution of omnichannel logistics:

- **Technological Advancements:** Innovations in artificial intelligence (AI), machine learning (ML), and the Internet of Things (IoT) are enabling more sophisticated logistics operations. These technologies help optimize inventory management, enhance demand forecasting, and streamline last-mile delivery processes.

- **Increased Consumer Demand for Convenience:** Modern consumers value convenience above all else. They expect businesses to offer a range of delivery and pickup options, such as same-day delivery, curbside pickup, and buy-online-pickup-in-store (BOPIS).

- **Rising Competition:** With the growth of e-commerce giants like Amazon and Alibaba, the competitive landscape has intensified. To stay competitive, businesses must adopt agile logistics strategies that can quickly respond to market changes and consumer preferences.

- **Sustainability Considerations:** As environmental concerns gain prominence, consumers are increasingly looking for sustainable shopping options. Businesses that can offer eco-friendly delivery solutions, such as green packaging or carbon-neutral shipping, are likely to gain a competitive edge.

CHAPTER 5 FUTURE TRENDS AND INNOVATIONS IN SUPPLY CHAIN MANAGEMENT

The Role of Technology in Shaping the Future of Omnichannel Logistics

Technology is at the heart of the future of e-commerce and omnichannel logistics. Companies are leveraging cutting-edge tools to enhance efficiency, reduce costs, and provide superior customer experiences. Key technological trends include

- **AI and Machine Learning:** AI and ML are transforming logistics by enabling more accurate demand forecasting, optimizing delivery routes, and enhancing inventory management. For example, AI-powered algorithms can analyze vast amounts of data to predict consumer demand patterns, allowing businesses to maintain optimal stock levels and minimize waste.

- **Robotics and Automation:** Automation is revolutionizing warehouse operations. Robots are now capable of handling various tasks, from picking and packing to sorting and inventory management. Automated warehouses can operate around the clock with minimal human intervention, significantly reducing labor costs and improving efficiency.

- **Blockchain Technology:** Blockchain is emerging as a powerful tool for enhancing supply chain transparency and security. By providing a decentralized ledger of all transactions, blockchain can help reduce fraud, ensure product authenticity, and streamline cross-border logistics.

- **IoT and Smart Sensors:** IoT devices and smart sensors are being used to track goods in real time, monitor environmental conditions during transit, and manage inventory more effectively. This technology allows businesses to maintain end-to-end visibility over their supply chains, enhancing operational efficiency and reducing the risk of disruptions.

Emerging Trends in E-commerce and Omnichannel Logistics

As the e-commerce landscape continues to evolve, several key trends are likely to shape the future of omnichannel logistics:

- **Hyperpersonalization:** The next frontier in e-commerce is hyperpersonalization, where businesses use advanced analytics and AI to deliver highly tailored shopping experiences. This could include personalized product recommendations, customized marketing messages, and dynamic pricing based on individual consumer behavior.

- **Micro-Fulfillment Centers:** To meet the growing demand for faster delivery, businesses are increasingly turning to micro-fulfillment centers—small, automated warehouses located close to urban centers. These facilities enable rapid order processing and delivery, reducing last-mile delivery times and costs.

- **Direct-to-Consumer (DTC) Models:** The DTC model is gaining traction as businesses look to bypass traditional retail channels and sell directly to consumers. This approach allows companies to build stronger relationships with customers, gain better control over their brand, and capture higher profit margins.

- **Sustainable Logistics Solutions:** As environmental concerns become more pressing, businesses are exploring innovative ways to reduce their carbon footprint. This includes investing in electric delivery vehicles, using biodegradable packaging materials, and optimizing delivery routes to minimize fuel consumption.

- **Contactless Delivery:** The COVID-19 pandemic has accelerated the adoption of contactless delivery options. In the future, we can expect to see more businesses offering contactless delivery services, utilizing technologies such as drones and autonomous vehicles to ensure safe, efficient, and reliable delivery.

Examples of Companies Leading the Way in Omnichannel Logistics

Several companies are already making strides in the realm of omnichannel logistics, demonstrating how innovative strategies and technologies can enhance customer experiences and drive business growth:

- **Amazon:** Amazon is a pioneer in omnichannel logistics, continually setting new standards for delivery speed and convenience. The company's extensive network of fulfillment centers, coupled with its investment in robotics and automation, allows it to offer same-day and even two-hour delivery options in many areas. Amazon's use of AI and machine learning for demand forecasting and inventory management further enhances its ability to meet customer expectations.

- **Walmart:** Walmart has successfully integrated its online and offline channels to create a seamless shopping experience. The company's "Walmart+" membership program offers free delivery from its stores, and its robust BOPIS service allows customers to order online and pick up their purchases at their nearest store. Walmart has also invested heavily in automation and robotics to streamline its supply chain operations, reduce costs, and improve service levels.

- **Zara:** The fashion retailer Zara is known for its agile supply chain and rapid inventory turnover. Zara's omnichannel strategy includes a sophisticated inventory management system that provides real-time visibility into stock levels across all stores and distribution centers. This allows Zara to quickly respond to changing consumer trends and ensure that popular items are always available, whether customers shop online or in-store.

Challenges and Opportunities in the Future of Omnichannel Logistics

While the future of e-commerce and omnichannel logistics is full of promise, it also presents several challenges:

- **Supply Chain Complexity:** Integrating multiple sales channels and ensuring a seamless customer experience can be challenging, particularly for businesses with complex supply chains. Managing inventory, coordinating deliveries, and maintaining accurate data across all channels require sophisticated systems and robust collaboration between stakeholders.

- **Cybersecurity Risks:** As businesses become more reliant on digital technologies, they face increased cybersecurity risks. Protecting customer data, securing online transactions, and safeguarding supply chain information from cyber threats will be critical to maintaining customer trust and ensuring business continuity.

- **Adapting to Rapid Technological Changes:** Keeping up with the pace of technological advancements can be daunting. Businesses need to invest in new technologies, train their workforce, and continuously adapt their strategies to stay competitive in a rapidly evolving market.

However, these challenges also present opportunities for businesses to differentiate themselves. Companies that can effectively navigate these complexities and embrace innovation will be well-positioned to thrive in the future of e-commerce and omnichannel logistics.

5.12 Preparing for Future Disruptions in Supply Chains

From natural disasters and pandemics to geopolitical tensions and cyberattacks, the potential risks that could disrupt supply chains are numerous and constantly changing. Preparing for future disruptions requires a proactive, strategic approach that incorporates resilience, flexibility, and innovation into every aspect of supply chain management. This section explores how companies can effectively prepare for these disruptions by anticipating potential risks, building robust contingency plans, and leveraging cutting-edge technologies.

CHAPTER 5   FUTURE TRENDS AND INNOVATIONS IN SUPPLY CHAIN MANAGEMENT

Understanding the Landscape of Supply Chain Disruptions

To prepare for future disruptions, companies must first understand the myriad of risks that can impact their supply chains. These risks can be broadly categorized into three types: operational, strategic, and external.

- **Operational Risks:** These are internal to the company and include issues like equipment failure, labor strikes, or internal process failures. While these risks can often be controlled or mitigated through strong internal processes and maintenance schedules, they still require careful planning and monitoring.

- **Strategic Risks:** These risks relate to the decisions made by a company's leadership and can include mergers and acquisitions, shifts in supplier strategy, or changes in product lines. These risks require alignment between supply chain strategy and overall business strategy to ensure that the supply chain can support the company's objectives.

- **External Risks**: External risks are those that originate outside the company and are often the most challenging to predict and manage. They include natural disasters, geopolitical events, pandemics, and cyber threats. These risks can disrupt supply chains in various ways, such as delaying shipments, increasing costs, or reducing the availability of critical materials.

CHAPTER 5   FUTURE TRENDS AND INNOVATIONS IN SUPPLY CHAIN MANAGEMENT

Building a Resilient Supply Chain

Resilience is the ability of a supply chain to anticipate, adapt, and recover from disruptions. Building a resilient supply chain involves several key strategies:

- **Diversification of Suppliers:** Relying on a single supplier or a limited number of suppliers for critical components is a significant risk. To mitigate this, companies should diversify their supplier base across different regions and consider having multiple suppliers for key products. For example, during the COVID-19 pandemic, companies with a diverse supplier base were better able to navigate the shutdowns in China and other parts of Asia by quickly shifting their sourcing to alternative suppliers in different regions.

- **Inventory Management:** Holding strategic reserves of critical inventory can help cushion the impact of supply chain disruptions. This does not mean overstocking, which can tie up valuable capital and increase storage costs, but rather carefully managing safety stock levels based on risk assessments. Companies like Apple, which maintain strategic stockpiles of critical components, have demonstrated how effective inventory management can mitigate risks associated with supplier disruptions.

- **Supply Chain Visibility:** Achieving end-to-end visibility across the supply chain allows companies to quickly identify and respond to potential disruptions. This involves leveraging technologies such as IoT

CHAPTER 5   FUTURE TRENDS AND INNOVATIONS IN SUPPLY CHAIN MANAGEMENT

sensors, advanced analytics, and blockchain to monitor supply chain activities in real time. For instance, Maersk, a global leader in container shipping, uses IoT and blockchain technologies to provide real-time tracking of cargo and enhance visibility across its supply chain, enabling faster response to potential disruptions.

Enhancing Flexibility in Supply Chain Operations

Flexibility is the ability to quickly adapt to changing conditions and is crucial for mitigating the impact of disruptions. Companies can enhance flexibility through several approaches:

- **Agile Supply Chain Practices:** Implementing agile practices, such as just-in-time (JIT) inventory management and rapid response teams, allows companies to quickly adjust to changes in demand or supply. Agile supply chains are characterized by their ability to pivot quickly and efficiently, whether it's to respond to a sudden increase in demand or to source alternative materials when a primary supplier is disrupted.

- **Dynamic Network Optimization:** Using advanced analytics and machine learning algorithms, companies can dynamically optimize their supply chain networks in real time. This allows them to make data-driven decisions about sourcing, production, and distribution in response to changing conditions. For example, Unilever has implemented advanced analytics to dynamically adjust its supply chain operations based on real-time data, improving its ability to respond to disruptions and changing market conditions.

- **Modular Production Systems:** Modular production systems, where products are designed in interchangeable modules, allow for more flexibility in production and assembly processes. This approach enables companies to quickly switch production lines or change product configurations in response to disruptions or shifts in demand.

Leveraging Technology for Disruption Preparedness

The rapid advancement of technology is providing new tools and techniques for preparing for supply chain disruptions:

- **Predictive Analytics and Artificial Intelligence:** Predictive analytics and AI can help companies anticipate potential disruptions before they occur. By analyzing vast amounts of data from various sources, these technologies can identify patterns and trends that may indicate a potential risk. For instance, AI algorithms can analyze weather data, political news, and social media to predict potential disruptions and allow companies to take proactive measures.

- **Digital Twins:** A digital twin is a virtual model of a supply chain that can be used to simulate different scenarios and test responses to various disruptions. By creating a digital twin of their supply chain, companies can experiment with different strategies and identify the most effective ways to respond to potential disruptions. Companies like Siemens are using digital twins to optimize their supply chain operations and improve their ability to respond to disruptions.

- **Blockchain for Enhanced Transparency and Security:** Blockchain technology can provide enhanced transparency and security in supply chains by creating a decentralized ledger of all transactions. This can help reduce fraud, ensure the authenticity of products, and improve traceability. For example, IBM's Food Trust blockchain network is being used by companies like Walmart to improve transparency and traceability in their food supply chains, enhancing their ability to quickly identify and respond to potential disruptions.

Developing Robust Contingency Plans

Contingency planning is a critical aspect of preparing for supply chain disruptions. It involves identifying potential risks, developing response strategies, and conducting regular drills and simulations to ensure readiness:

- **Scenario Planning:** Companies should develop multiple scenarios for potential disruptions and create detailed response plans for each. These scenarios should cover a range of possibilities, from minor disruptions to major catastrophes, and include strategies for communication, decision-making, and resource allocation.

- **Crisis Management Teams:** Establishing dedicated crisis management teams with clearly defined roles and responsibilities can help ensure a swift and coordinated response to disruptions. These teams should be trained regularly and equipped with the tools and resources needed to manage crises effectively.

- **Regular Drills and Simulations:** Conducting regular drills and simulations can help companies test their contingency plans and identify any weaknesses or gaps. This ensures that all employees are familiar with their roles and responsibilities in the event of a disruption and that the company is prepared to respond effectively.

The Role of Collaboration and Partnership in Mitigating Disruptions

Collaboration and partnership are essential for preparing for supply chain disruptions. Companies must work closely with their suppliers, customers, and other stakeholders to build a resilient and flexible supply chain:

- **Supplier Collaboration:** Building strong relationships with suppliers and engaging in regular communication can help companies identify potential risks and develop joint strategies for mitigating them. Collaborative forecasting and planning with suppliers can also help ensure that both parties are prepared for potential disruptions.

- **Industry Partnerships:** Collaborating with industry partners and participating in industry forums can provide valuable insights into emerging risks and best practices for managing disruptions. Industry partnerships can also facilitate information sharing and joint initiatives to improve supply chain resilience.

- **Government and Community Engagement:** Engaging with government agencies and local communities can help companies better understand the regulatory environment and potential risks in different regions. It can also facilitate access to critical resources and support in the event of a disruption.

Index

A

Advanced analytics, 11, 31, 58, 81, 110, 123, 151
Agility, 20, 52, 82, 91, 123
AI-based quality control systems, 126
AI-driven analytics, 47
AI-driven vision systems, 126
AI-powered predictive analytics, 2, 8, 10, 39
AI-powered tools, 82, 120
Alibaba, 65, 149
Amazon's logistics network, 9
Analytical hierarchy process (AHP), 71
Artificial intelligence (AI), 10, 52, 63, 72, 92
  logistics and transportation, 125
  ML
    customer experiences, 128
    data-driven approach, 128
    development and deployment, 129
    supply chain management, 129
    tools, 129
  supply chain management, 125
  Unilever, 125

Automated guided vehicles (AGVs), 13, 32
Automated storage and retrieval systems (AS/RS), 62
Automated warehouses, 62, 65, 150
Automation, 11, 32, 53, 120, 150
Automotive industry, 82, 92
Automotive Industry Action Group (AIAG), 82, 104

B

Big data analytics, 11, 27, 28, 58, 135, 137, 139–141
  algorithms and tools, 135
  applications, 136
  customer-centric, 142
  in supply chain management, 136
  supply chains, 142
Blockchain technology, 11, 34, 52, 59, 72, 105, 110, 121, 130, 133–135, 150, 159
  benefits, 121, 131
  operational costs, 132
  Renault, 135
  supply chain efficiency, 131

INDEX

Blockchain technology (*cont.*)
   supply chain management, 130
   Unilever, 134
   Walmart, 131
Bullwhip effect, 2, 6, 106, 114

C

Capacity planning, 33
   balance flexibility and efficiency, 35
   on continuous improvement and data-driven insights, 36
   operations management, 33
   semiconductor manufacturer, 33
   strategic investment, 35
   techniques, effective capacity planning, 34
Carrier management, 55
Climate-controlled warehouses, 62
Coca-Cola's collaborative logistics strategy, 116
Collaboration, 15, 41, 83–117, 160
Collaborative approach, 42, 92, 97, 112, 117
Collaborative distribution centers (CDCs), 115
Collaborative forecasting, 28, 29, 160
Collaborative logistics, 58, 115–116

Collaborative Planning, Forecasting, and Replenishment (CPFR), 93, 114
   in action, 95
   benefits, 94
   collaboration agreement, 94
   collaboration—bringing, 94
   dynamic market environment, 97
   effectiveness, 96
   future, 97
   inventory planning and replenishment, 96
   performance, 97
   practices, 95
   sharing data and forecasts, 113
   traditional approach, 94
Consumer electronics market, 92
Contingency planning, 159
Continuous improvement, 36, 41, 116
Cost reduction, 8, 90
Counterfeiting, 132
   Maersk, 133
   Pfizer, 132
   supplier relationship management, 134
   supply chain, 132
   traceability, 133
Customer service, 51
Customization, 123
Cyberattacks, 107, 154
Cybersecurity risks, 154

INDEX

D

Data-driven approach, 138
Decision-making, 86
Demand-driven inventory optimization, 31
Demand forecasting, 50, 51
    big data for real-time insights, 27
    collaborative forecasting, 28, 29
    leverage ML, 27
    predictive analytics, strategic decision-making, 28
    scenario planning, 29
Digitalization, 120
Digital tools, 47
Digital transformation, 120
Digital twin, 158
Direct-to-consumer (DTC) Models, 151
Distributed ledger technology (DLT), 130
Distribution centers, 63
Distribution management, 46
    distribution channels, 46
    rise of e-commerce, 47
Distribution network design, 66
    factors
        cost, 68
        customer demand, 68
        level of service, 68
        supply chain resilience, 69
        sustainability, 69
    impacted technologies
        AI, 72
        blockchain, 72
        IoT, 72
        3D printing, 72
    methodologies, 69
        AHP, 71
        optimization models, 70
        simulation, 70
    strategic importance, 67
    Unilever, 71
    Zara's distribution network, 71
Dynamic scheduling system, 26

E

E-commerce, 122, 148, 150
Effective resource allocation, 26
Electronic components, 126
Environmental, social, and governance (ESG), 134

F, G

Failure mode and effects analysis (FMEA), 108
Fast-paced market environment, 95
FedEx, 49
Flexibility, 157
    agile supply chains, 157
    data-driven decisions, 157
    modular production systems, 158

INDEX

Fourth-party logistics (4PL)
    AI and big data analytics, 75
    key advantage, 75
    4PL model, 76
    provider, 75
    as supply chain integrator, 75
    and 3PL, 74
    value-added services, 77
Future disruptions
    external risks, 155
    risks, 155
    operational Risks, 155
    strategic risk, 155

H

Hyperpersonalization, 151

I

IBM's collaborative innovation, 116
IBM Supply Chain Intelligence Suite, 127
Information sharing, 103
    barriers, 104
    benefits, 103
    and coordination, 106
    cost savings, 106
    inventory levels, 106
    operational benefits, 106
    standardized data, 104
Integrated supply chain (ISC), 92, 116

Internet of Things (IoT), 11, 31, 52, 63
Inventory management, 6, 29, 50, 96
    automation, role, 32
    demand-driven inventory optimization, 31
    effective management, 29
    goals, 30
    integration of technology, 31
    JIT inventory management, 30
    real-time data analytics, 30
    sustainable inventory management practices, 32
IoT devices, 47, 120, 150
IoT sensors, 39

J

Just-in-time (JIT), 2, 6, 30, 37, 114, 115

K

Kaizen, 41
Key performance indicators (KPIs), 100

L

Lean manufacturing
    principles, 38, 39
    continuous improvement, 41
    elimination of waste, 40

INDEX

pull production systems, 42
respect and empower
people, 42
value stream mapping, 42, 43
Load optimization, 56
Logistics and distribution
management, 45, 46
Logistics management, 46, 48
balancing cost and service
quality, 46
components
customer service, 51
inventory management, 50
order fulfillment, 50
reverse logistics, 51
transportation
management, 49
warehousing, 50
demand forecasting and
planning, 50, 51
role and importance, 48, 49
technological innovations
artificial intelligence (AI), 52
automation and robotics, 53
blockchain, 52
Internet of Things (IoT), 52
machine learning (ML), 52

M

Machine learning (ML), 27, 52, 63
Micro-fulfillment centers, 151
Modular production
systems, 158

N

NexaTech supply chain, 17–21

O

Omnichannel logistics, 149
Amazon, 152
competitive landscape, 149
consumers value
convenience, 149
e-commerce, 153
sustainable shopping
options, 149
technological advancements, 149
Walmart, 153
Zara, 153
Operational risks, 108
Order fulfillment, 50

P, Q

Predictive analytics, 28, 158
Predictive and prescriptive
analytics, 141
Private warehouses, 62
Procter & Gamble (P&G), 51, 100,
111, 113
Production planning, 25
dynamic production
scheduling, 26
resource allocation, 25, 26
scheduling, 25
Production planning and control
(PPC), 24

INDEX

Production scheduling, 24, 26, 36
    effective scheduling, 36
    innovative approaches, 36
    strategies, 37
        continuous improvement and adaptability, 39, 40
        finite capacity, 37
        integration of advanced technologies, 39
        JIT scheduling, 37
        lean manufacturing principles, 38, 39
        real-time monitoring and control, 38
        resource optimization, 37
        sequencing and prioritization, 37
Public warehouses, 61
Pull production systems, 42

R

Radio frequency identification (RFID), 31
Resilience, 156
    inventory, 156
    strategies, 156
    supplier, 156
    visibility, 156
Resilient
    agility, 123
    digital twins, 123
    regionalization, 123
Resource allocation, 26

Reverse logistics, 51, 77
    challenges, 81
    components
        asset recovery, 80
        recycling and disposal, 79, 80
        remanufacturing and refurbishment, 79
        returns management, 78, 79
        waste management, 80
    effective logistics, 78
    innovative strategies, 81, 82
    online shopping, 78
    sustainability, 82
Risk identification and assessment, 109
Risk management, 111, 139
    IBM, 139
    personalized customer experience, 140
    supply chain, 139
Risk mitigation, 109
Robotics, 11, 53

S

Scenario planning, 29
Smartphones, 4, 24, 79
Supplier collaboration, 138
Supplier relationship management (SRM)
    advancements, 101
    artificial intelligence, 102
    benefits, 99
    enhanced, 127, 138

foundation, 99
goal, 98
information sharing and coordination, 102
innovation, 100
iPhone, 99
performance monitoring, 101
risk management, 98
scorecards, 100
strategic partners, 98
supplier performance and accountability, 100
Toyota's relationship, 98
trust and accountability, 101
Supply chain, 4
complexity, 153
disruptions, 5, 158
global supply chain, 4
integration, 84, 93
simple supply chain, 4
smartphone, 4
Supply chain integration
automotive manufacturer, 86
benefits, 87
cohesive, 84
collaboration, 87
and communication, 90
components, 90
cross-functional teams, 86
customer satisfaction, 88
effective communication and data sharing, 85
efficiency, 90
forecasting and inventory management, 91
global electronics manufacturer, 84
innovation, 89
inventory levels and production, 90
mitigate risks, 88
pharmaceutical company, 87
relationships, 86
responsive, 88
solution, 89
standardizing processes, 86
strategies, 85
technology, 85
Supply chain management (SCM), 1, 3, 101, 107, 116, 117, 136
case studies
Amazon, 13
NexaTech, 17–21
Toyota, 14
Zara, 12, 13
concepts
bullwhip effect, 6
inventory management, 6
JIT inventory, 6
lead time, 5
supply chain visibility, 5
effective SCM, 1
evolution, 2, 7–9
future, 124

INDEX

Supply chain management (SCM) (*cont.*)
   mid-sized electronics manufacturer
      advanced inventory management, 15, 16
      challenges, 15
      smart logistics and transportation optimization, 16
      supplier consolidation and collaboration, 15
   modern SCM, 2
   role of technology, 10
      advanced analytics and big data, 11
      artificial intelligence (AI), 10
      blockchain technology, 11
      innovations, 10
      Internet of Things (IoT), 11
      robotics and automation, 11
   Zara, 2
Supply chain operations, 122
Supply chain performance, 134
Supply chain risk management, 108, 110, 127
Supply chains, 107, 146, 154
Sustainability, 32, 47, 57, 58, 69, 121, 142
   consumers demand, 143
   cost savings, 143
   regulations, 142
   supply chain process, 142

Sustainable Agriculture Code (SAC), 112
Sustainable Agriculture Initiative (SAI), 112
Sustainable inventory management practices, 32
Sustainable packaging solutions, 122
Sustainable sourcing, 113
Sustainable supply chain practices
   components, 144
   energy consumption, 143
   environmental concerns, 147
   green logistics, 144
   IKEA, 145
   management, 147
   Patagonia, 145
   practices, 146, 147
   profitability, 146
   social responsibility, 144
   stakeholders, 142, 146
   sustainable practices, 146
   sustainably sourcing, 143
   Unilever, 144
   waste materials, 143
Sustainable transportation management, 57
Sustainable warehousing practices, 64

T

Technology, 105, 110, 150
   blockchain, 105
   cloud-based platforms, 105

global shipping giant, 105
IoT devices, 105
Tesla, 65
Third-party logistics (3PL)
    logistics activities, 73
    primary advantages, 74
    success, 76
    success model, 76
    value-added services, 77
    warehousing and distribution needs, 73
3D printing, 65, 72
Toyota Production System (TPS), 40
Traditional demand forecasting methods, 24
Transportation and logistics, 138
Transportation
    management, 49, 53
    components
        carrier selection and management, 55
        freight consolidation, 55, 56
        load optimization, 56
        real-time tracking, 56
        real-time visibility, 57
        sustainability, 57
        transportation planning, 54
    globalization and e-commerce, 53
    impactful technologies, 58
        autonomous vehicles and drones, 59
        big data and analytics, 58
        blockchain, 59
        TMS platforms, 58
    supply chain agility, 54
    transportation costs, 53
Transportation management systems (TMS), 16, 55, 58

U

United Parcel Service (UPS), 138

V

Value stream mapping, 42, 43

W, X, Y

Warehousing, 50, 60, 61
    automated warehouses, 62
    climate-controlled warehouses, 62
    distribution centers, 63
    private warehouses, 62
    public warehouses, 61
    role, 61
    value-added services, 61
Warehousing and storage
    AI and ML, 63
    blockchain, 64
    IoT, 63
    real-world applications, 65, 66
    sustainable warehousing, 64
    3D printing, 65
Waste management, 80

INDEX

Z

Zara, 2
Zara's business model, 12

Zara's data-driven approach, 137
Zara's distribution network, 13
Zara's supply chain strategy, 13

MIX
Papier aus verantwortungsvollen Quellen
Paper from responsible sources
FSC® C105338

If you have any concerns about our products,
you can contact us on
ProductSafety@springernature.com

In case Publisher is established outside the EU,
the EU authorized representative is:
Springer Nature Customer Service Center GmbH
Europaplatz 3, 69115 Heidelberg, Germany

Printed by Libri Plureos GmbH
in Hamburg, Germany